Companions

Companions

Accompanying Newcomers into Church Life and Faith

Marney Ault Wasserman

Foreword by Sue Westfall

WIPF & STOCK · Eugene, Oregon

COMPANIONS
Accompanying Newcomers into Church Life and Faith

Copyright © 2016 Marney Ault Wasserman. All rights reserved. Except for brief quotations in critical publications or reviews, no part of this book may be reproduced in any manner without prior written permission from the publisher. Write: Permissions, Wipf and Stock Publishers, 199 W. 8th Ave., Suite 3, Eugene, OR 97401.

Unless otherwise noted, all biblical quotations with the exception of the Psalms are taken from the New Revised Standard Version Bible, copyright © 1989, Division of Christian Education of the National Council of the Churches of Christ in the United States of America. Used by permission. All rights reserved.

Quotations from the Psalms are from *An Inclusive-Language Psalter for the Christian People*, edited by Gordon Lathrop and Gail Ramshaw, copyright © 1993 by the Order of Saint Benedict. Published by Liturgical Press, Collegeville, Minnesota. Used with permission.

Additional biblical quotations, as noted, are taken from:

The Holy Bible, Today's New International Version ®, TNIV®, copyright © 2001, 2015 by Biblica, Inc™. Used by permission of Zondervan. All rights reserved worldwide.

The Message, copyright © 1993, 1994, 1995, 1996, 2000, 2001, 2002 by Eugene H. Peterson. Used by permission of NavPress. All rights reserved. Represented by Tyndale House Publishers, Inc.

Wipf & Stock
An Imprint of Wipf and Stock Publishers
199 W. 8th Ave., Suite 3
Eugene, OR 97401

www.wipfandstock.com

PAPERBACK ISBN: 978-1-5326-0092-0
HARDCOVER ISBN: 978-1-5326-0094-4
EBOOK ISBN: 978-1-5326-0093-7

Manufactured in the U.S.A.   10/28/16

Dedicated with gratitude, to the members and leaders
of Trinity Presbyterian Church, Tucson, Arizona,
who were willing to try a new idea and grow with it;

and to David, my husband and colleague in ministry,
who is my greatest encourager.

Contents

Foreword by Sue Westfall | ix
Preface | xi
Acknowledgments | xiii

1 The Context | 1

2 The Values | 4
    Friendship | 4
    Hospitality | 5
    Spirituality | 6
    Transformation | 7
    Discernment | 9
    Community | 10
    Baptism | 11

3 The Conversations | 13
    1. Vocation: The Rhythms of Living | 14
    2. Prayer: A Way of Knowing God | 14
    3. Forgiveness: A Way of Loving Neighbors | 15
    4. Gratitude: A Way of Living with Things | 15
    A. Scripture: The Story and Our Stories | 16
    B. Belief: Who Is This Jesus? | 16
    5. Community: Belonging to One Another | 17
    6. Calling: Sent to Serve the World | 17

4 The Methods | 19
    Conversation | 19
    Prayer | 21
    Member Companions: Getting Started | 23

Newcomers: Matching and Encouraging | 24
Lectio Divina | 25
Flexibility and Adaptation | 27
Pastoral and Other Leadership | 29

5 The Materials | 32
Welcome to *Companions*! | 33
Member Companion Guidelines | 36
The Conversations | 41
Daily Prayer Card | 51
Contact Information Form | 52

6 The Backstory | 53
Compañeros in Tucson, Arizona | 53
Closing the "Back Door" | 55
A Festival of Faith | 56
Strengthening the Faith of the Church | 57

Appendix: Resources for Leaders | 61
Member Companion Training Session | 61
Group Gathering A: The Bible as One Story | 66
Group Gathering B: What We Believe | 69
Lectio Divina: A Simple Process for Doing *Lectio Divina* in a Group | 74
Baptismal Preparation Session | 77
Sample Letters and Publicity | 81
   Sample Letter to Recent Visitors | 82
   Sample Invitation to Member Companion Training | 83
   Sample Newsletter or Website Publicity | 85
   Sample Sunday Reminders or Announcements | 87
Church Council Meeting to Receive New Members | 89
Liturgies | 91
   Introduction of Companions in Faith | 92
   Renewal of Baptism | 94
Additional Conversation Guides | 99
   Worship | 100
   Discipleship | 101
   Service | 102
   Justice | 103

Bibliography | 105

Foreword

WHAT A PRIVILEGE IT is for me to write this foreword to Marney's terrific book, *Companions*. When I worked as the Presbytery Pastor for the Presbytery de Cristo, my office was located in Trinity Presbyterian Church in Tucson, Arizona, where Marney developed and used this model of accompanying newcomers into the faith and life of the church. We were frequent conversation partners and I have learned much from this wise and effective pastor. Then, while the congregation was using this approach, I had opportunity to speak with participants; the stories they shared were powerful and moving. I sensed a spirited "buzz" in the congregation as people began openly sharing with one another, and with the "others," the love, grace, and power of Christ, alive and visible in their very midst. This is a book that can change the culture of your congregation!

I'm sure I wasn't the only person who encouraged Marney to make this invaluable resource available to the whole church, but I am certainly one of them. *Companions* is, at its simplest, a relational method of visitor/new member integration. With theological depth and eloquence, Marney has called upon the church's ancient values such as community, hospitality, sacred friendship, and baptismal identity to foster conversations about the things that really matter. Sadly, such conversations aren't happening enough in our churches, resulting in church members who are not actively growing in their own life of faith and who are reluctant to share their faith with others. So do you want to integrate visitors and new members meaningfully into the life of the congregation? *Check.* Do you want to develop the congregation's capacity to see God at work in their life and share their faith with others? *Check.* Do you want your congregants to be formed in Christ and not just informed about Christ? *Check.* Do you want your congregation to reclaim its missional vision? *Check.* Do you want to form a people who bear lively, authentic witness to God's ongoing work to save the

Foreword

world? *Check.* Honestly. This book (with a dose of the Spirit, who is ready and able!) opens pathways for all of that to happen in your congregation.

Although *Companions* was written as an innovative and effective approach to "companioning" newcomers into the life of Christ's body in the world, its scope and depth make it much more than that. Here Marney has addressed two of the church's most vexing challenges —evangelism and discipleship—and offered up a single, elegant method of inviting Christians to talk about Christ, to love those whom Christ loves, and to witness to abundant life in him. This book can revitalize your congregation's life, in dozens of different ways, because the model is just that thorough, accessible, and relevant.

Thank you, Marney, for offering the church this catalyst for growing passionate, practicing disciples of Jesus who are equipped and eager to share their lively faith with one another and the world, becoming ever more transparent and authentic witnesses to the world-saving love of God in Jesus Christ.

Rev. Dr. Sue Westfall
Director of Curriculum and Mentoring, Macedonian Ministry

Preface

THIS BOOK CAME ABOUT from the simple desire to share with others in the church an idea that worked amazingly well in a congregation I served. It was a new way of doing ministry with newcomers to the church, and it ended up reshaping the life of the congregation in significant ways. While I'm a firm believer that there is no such thing as a "magic, whistling bullet" in ministry (the notion that a program that worked well in my church will necessarily work well in yours too), I'm convinced that *Companions* is a model worth sharing with the church.

It will naturally function a little differently in different congregations, but *Companions* points in what I believe are needed new directions for the church's ministry with newcomers and for the work of church growth. *Companions* is relational and flexible. It's built around simple human conversation. It takes the faith seriously, and at the same time is deeply respectful of people and their varied experiences. It's grounded in ancient biblical values and core spiritual practices. It exercises and strengthens the faith of the whole congregation.

The bottom line is this: it has never mattered more that we in the church live out our life together as a spiritually hospitable people. This resource is an attempt to show at least one concrete way congregations may build into their common life practices of spiritual hospitality—offering a genuine hand of friendship and the rich gifts of the Christian faith to those who come looking for something of God in our midst. It is my hope that you will find ways to use it to that end, and that your congregation will grow in its capacity for gracious welcome, profound hospitality, and lively faith.

Acknowledgments

THIS BOOK WOULD NOT have come about apart from the willingness of the congregation at Trinity Presbyterian Church in Tucson, Arizona, to take a risk and try a new ministry. It was for this church that the *Companions* process was created, and among them that it was tried, practiced, improved upon, and developed. I am indebted to the church's pioneer newcomers and member companions, who in those first two years launched eagerly into the conversations, and became staunch supporters of the companioning process, including: Ron Acosta, Peggy Andrews, Jo Baker, Bev Bechtel, Jan Bond, Lori Boston, Holly Clark, Dave Croteau, Jason De Pizzo and Jennifer Lohse, Valerie Dorr, Jon Dyhr, Faye Foxx, Nancy Hamadou, Dave and Pat Hardy, Tom and Vade Henderson, Debbie Hobbs, David and Beth Holliday, Annika Jones, Pat and Carroll Keegstra, Rosemary Krivel, Heather Lind, Heather Mace and Travis Spillers, Drea Nelson, Chuck and Sally Riester, Kiwon Sohn and Suhyon Noh, Alice Smedley, Wayne Steele, Autumn and Jacob Witt, and Bobby Whipple.

In addition, I am doubly indebted to Nancy Hamadou, who became my "right hand" in developing the *Companions* ministry at Trinity. Nancy was among the first group of trained member companions, and served ably in that capacity for at least half a dozen newcomers. Within a year or two, she had taken on the coordinating tasks that would help keep the new companioning ministry running smoothly. She contacted visitors, did the companion matching, coordinated calendars, and stayed in touch with everyone involved. She and I took turns leading the group meetings, and worked together periodically to evaluate and edit the conversation guides. In short, her leadership gifts and her steady support as *Companions* coordinator were invaluable in the success of this ministry.

A doctoral research project by the Rev. Bart Roush, then serving Fox Valley Presbyterian Church in Geneva, Illinois, as an associate pastor, first

Acknowledgments

suggested the language to distinguish between "information-based" and "discernment-based" new member processes. Bart visited Trinity Presbyterian Church in the spring of 2011, and later shared with us his research on a small handful of churches, Trinity included, that were exploring alternatives to the "new member class" and developing more "discernment-based" approaches to working with newcomers and receiving new members. His thesis, submitted to Luther Seminary in St. Paul, Minnesota, in 2012, and entitled "Incorporating Adults toward a Missional Imagination: A Study of Four Congregations," was concerned with demonstrating that such discernment-based membership processes contributed to more highly missional churches. While his conclusions from such a small sample were limited, his focus on alternative membership processes and newcomer ministries was informative and encouraging.

Numerous others provided support and help along the way, both for the *Companions* ministry and for the compiling of its story and resources into this book. Tucson colleagues Bill Voigt, Harriet Marsh, Lynn Moser, and Sue Westfall were unfailingly encouraging of the companioning ministry at Trinity. Pastoral colleagues who expressed an interest in trying out some of these resources early on included Christie Gravely (Easley, SC), Craig Reynolds (Scottsdale, AZ), Fred Anderson (New York, NY), John Nelsen (El Paso, TX), Shannon Kershner (Chicago, IL), and probably a few others whose names I neglected to write down. Ministry colleagues Stan Ott (Vital Churches Institute) and David Maxwell (Presbyterian Publishing House) read early drafts of the manuscript and offered many valuable comments and suggestions. In addition, several others saw parts of the manuscript in progress and provided kind encouragement, including Emily Brink (Calvin Institute of Christian Worship), Ned Dewire (Methodist Theological School in Ohio), Kim Long (Columbia Theological Seminary), and David Gambrell (Presbyterian Church Office of Theology, Worship and Evangelism).

Finally, my thanks go to my husband David, who for three years served the Trinity congregation with me as co-pastor. It was David who nurtured the germ of an idea for a companioning ministry with newcomers, and encouraged me to create it. More recently, he has supported my work in writing and publishing this manuscript, and shares my hope that it will be a good gift to the church.

1

The Context

People come to the church today from widely different experiences, bringing with them different needs, expectations, and hopes. Some have been lifelong churchgoers and are simply looking for a new church home in a new community. Some have no Christian background at all, but find themselves curious about Jesus or drawn to the community of his followers. Some were raised in a church, but left it behind, and wonder if there might still be a place for them somewhere. Some return to raise their children in the faith, but are not sure what, if anything, the church has to offer to them as parents and young adults. Some were Catholic or Baptist or something else once, and want to see whether Presbyterian, Methodist, Episcopal, or another church may be a better fit. Some have been excluded, let down, even hurt by the church, so they're wary, yet longing to reconnect and find a place among God's people.

The people who enter the church's doors for the first time, those who sign our visitor pads or check the "wish to join" box, may know the Bible well, or not at all, or somewhere in between. They may have a rich prayer life, or none to speak of. They may be accustomed to the patterns of the church's worship, or find them strange and bewildering. They may be hoping to find a congregation just like their last one, or eager to get away from "that kind of church." Or they may know nothing at all of church life except what they hear in the news media or glimpse from a distance in the public arena. But as a group their circumstances, their experiences, and their spiritual needs are often widely different.

Companions

Just a few decades ago, the variety of newcomers approaching our doors was not so great. Most were at least cradle Christians, if not cradle Lutherans, Reformed, Congregationalists, Disciples, or (*fill in your denomination*). But the world has been changing around us. North American culture has become more diverse, more secular, less Christian, less faith oriented. So the question has become increasingly urgent: how can the church respond to the people beyond our doors and connect with their spiritual hunger and their widely varied faith experience?

For many decades, the standard option for interested visitors in the vast majority of Protestant congregations has been the "new member class" or "pastor's class": *come to this class or series of classes, and we'll tell you everything you need to know about what it means to be a member of this congregation, and this denomination.* In a widely Christian culture, this was a workable model. But in today's context, the new member class no longer serves so well. It's a one-size-fits-all program for an increasingly diverse group of potential participants. It's focused on denominational identity or congregational practices, when many around us are just trying to understand what it means to be Christian. It's typically too much about the church, and not enough about the God people come thirsty to know. It's designed to impart *in*formation, when so many come eager for tangible *trans*formation in their lives. It's generally structured as the means to a presumably desired end—church membership—but many today are wary of "joining," preferring a more open-ended opportunity to explore the spiritual life, theological thinking, religious practices, and church culture. And the "Pastor's Class," as it is called in some settings, is not surprisingly often pastor-centered, while the relationships that foster long-term congregational commitment are those built with other churchgoers—relationships through which newcomers can become part of a community and find a solid place among God's people.

Companions offers a different model for receiving new members and ministering to worship visitors. At its core, it is not a class, but a companioning process—pairing visitors interested in exploring a deeper commitment to Christ and his church with member companions already active in the life of the congregation. They meet for eight conversations about Christian faith and discipleship; these are scheduled at their own pace, and at times and places of their own choosing. Conversation topics like vocation, community, prayer, or forgiveness invite mutual sharing that is grounded in Scripture, guided by reflection questions, and engaged with

The Context

prayer. And because the ultimate context is not a class, but a conversation, *Companions* nurtures friendships, meets newcomers wherever they are in their spiritual journey, and helps them take the next steps to grow in their life with God. This is an accompaniment model, a mentoring or apprenticeship practice, rather than a classroom model. It's more relational, more spiritually centered, more open-ended, and more flexible than the average new member class. And in addition to encouraging the faith of those who come seeking, *Companions* also strengthens the faith of the church members who serve as their partners, and ultimately the faith and witness of the whole congregation.

Companions also offers a different model for encouraging church growth. Two core theological convictions about the church's work of evangelism are worth noting in this regard. First, church growth is the Spirit's work, not ours. As the apostle Paul once reminded the Corinthians, we do the watering and the nurturing, but it's God who gives the growth (1 Corinthians 3:7). When we do our work of welcome and witness and nurture, we're simply providing the Spirit with another occasion to transform lives—both the lives of those around us and our own. The second conviction is this: the reason the church needs to grow is never for its own sake. It's not because we need a larger membership roll, or some younger people, or new givers to help us meet our budget, or even just more people to keep us viable as a congregation. Rather the church needs to grow because there are people around us in need of rescue, people who are drowning in whatever sin or sorrow or hate or fear holds them captive, people who need the lifeline of God's love and mercy made real for them. *Companions* embodies both of these convictions by putting the emphasis on people over programs, on relationships over religious requirements, on the spiritual life over institutional assimilation. *Companions* also changes the focus, so that instead of just offering a procedure for visitors to join the church, a congregation can provide a service that (whether newcomers ultimately choose to seek church membership or not) helps them connect with others, connect with God, and grow spiritually.

2

The Values

EMBODIED IN THE DESIGN of *Companions* are core values that distinguish it from other more information-based approaches to worship visitors and prospective church members. Foremost among these is the value of friendship.

FRIENDSHIP

The Christian faith is fundamentally relational. We believe in the triune God—in the church's traditional language, Father, Son, and Holy Spirit—who share a life together as the one God. There is a relationship between Jesus, the God he calls *Abba*, and the Spirit that flows from and between and through them. Like the Trinity, which models a perfect divine community of three, the church is a community of many, where the quality of the relationships among us shapes who we are together and what we do as a people of God.

In John's Gospel, Jesus says to the Twelve, who have been his daily companions for three years, "*I do not call you servants any longer . . . but I have called you friends . . .*" (John 15:15). The disciples are friends because they are a part of Jesus, because he has chosen them and loved them, because there are no secrets between them and he gladly shares with them all that *Abba* gives. Friendship—deep, abiding friendship—is an important biblical metaphor for the church. Unlike family, who are united irrevocably by blood and by sometimes tangled emotional threads, friends are bound to one another by choice, by mutual commitment and loyalty and desire. Because Jesus calls us his friends, it is important in the church that we know and love one another as friends—friends of Christ and friends in Christ.

At its simplest, *Companions* works by building friendships. For newcomers to the church, an assigned member companion offers the possibility of a first friend, a place to start building one initial relationship that can lead to others and ultimately to finding a place in a community's life. Over several weeks of conversation, this one friendship has an opportunity to deepen, as two people share more of their lives with one another. While not all companions will become best friends, many will develop meaningful relationships that endure well beyond those first eight weeks of structured conversation.

The power of friendship emerges in other ways as well. Longtime church members, who can sometimes get stuck in their own familiar circles of church friends, discover that befriending a newcomer opens a new door in their own spiritual life. And tight little subgroups within the church become a bit more fluid and welcoming as they are stretched to include a visiting companion. Friendship also leads to strong, durable bonds, and fosters among newer members a long-term commitment to the church that is based not on the identity of its pastor or the quantity or quality of its programs, but on its people and the relationships that constitute a community.

HOSPITALITY

"Do not neglect to show hospitality to strangers, for by doing that some have entertained angels without knowing it" (Hebrews 13:2). Closely related to friendship is the value of hospitality. This means more than just being friendly and welcoming visitors to church, the way we might welcome guests in our home—although that in itself is a significant first step. But beyond making room for newcomers in our pews, Christian hospitality is about making room for new people in our lives. It's about being spiritually open with our stories, our time, our circles of friends, being ready to share with others our thinking about the faith, our experience of God, our practices of discipleship—not just on Sundays, but in parts of our Monday-to-Saturday world as well. It's about making a genuine place for people in our lives.

Jesus, of course, was a master at hospitality, although in the biblical record he was more often a guest than a host. Still, he was always attentive to individuals and their needs, observing with care and responding to each person, as an individual, in just the right way. Think of his unique encounters with Mary and with Martha in their home in Bethany (Luke 10:38–42), with Zaccheus the taxcollector in Jericho (Luke 19:1–10), or with the village children wherever he went (Mark 10:13–16, among others).

Companions is a ministry of hospitality. A warm greeting to a first-time visitor at the church door is a good beginning. Remembering that visitor by name or face a week later is important encouragement. For those who return looking for more, a member companion prepared to get to know and befriend that newcomer is a natural next step. Literally, hospitality means "the love of strangers." The capacity to welcome strangers into our lives requires both a clear sense of ourselves and the gifts we've been given, and a deep respect for all the "others" around us we do not yet know. It means being willing to be changed by the people we allow into our lives. By pairing active members with interested newcomers, *Companions* gives the church a concrete way to exercise its ministry of hospitality, and make a genuine and lasting place among us for the beloved strangers the Spirit of God is sending our way.

SPIRITUALITY

People who come to a church are usually looking for more than just a supportive community, more than a certain kind of worship or Bible Study or youth program or service opportunity. They are also hungry to fill a deeper spiritual need, whether they can name that need clearly or not. They may want to know God more, or understand the Bible better, or be stronger followers of Jesus. They may need to make sense out of an experience in their life that's been painful or troubling. They may need to forgive, or be forgiven. They may be looking for a prayer life they can sustain, a theology that makes sense, some personal experience of God's nearness. Even people who are just transferring their membership from one congregation to another will usually discover a spiritual dimension in their transition that's worth paying attention to.

Companions takes all these spiritual needs seriously, while acknowledging they differ depending on where we are in our lives and in our life with God. One newcomer and one member companion, talking together about the faith and the walk of discipleship, allows those deeper needs to surface and be addressed. Because the companioning conversations are one-on-one, they can begin where people are, focus on the things that matter most to each of them, and open the doors to honesty, exploration, intimacy, and growth—for both partners!

It sounds impossible, but somehow even in the church, where talking about our relationship with God ought to be the most natural thing in the world to do, we often don't. We talk easily enough about the church and its programs, about the Bible, or theological ideas; but we are hesitant, even with one another, to speak of our experience of God. We worry that our doubts will betray us as not true believers, or our lifestyles will show us up to be hypocrites, or our interest in the spiritual life will get us branded as way too holy to be any fun. *Companions* provides eight conversation guides that help people get focused on where God is in their lives and more comfortable with "God-speech."[1] They give two new friends a way to share some of the important spiritual dimensions of their lives, alongside the ordinary realities of work and family and everyday living.

Companions also has embedded within it the practice of several core spiritual disciplines. Attending Sunday worship together each week and praying daily for one another are key among these. Reading and reflection on Scripture is built into each of the conversations. So is prayer for and with each other—along with numerous suggestions to make praying together simple and accessible for people of varying Christian experience.

This emphasis on spiritual *practices*, rather than on spiritual understandings alone, aligns with the biblical record of the early church: *"They devoted themselves to the apostles' teaching and fellowship, to the breaking of bread and the prayers"* (Acts 2:42). Simple daily practices like theirs—study and fellowship, prayer and Scripture, worship and sacraments—are what believers do together in order to keep growing in grace, learning the faith, being transformed. They are also what believers do together to strengthen the community, build up the church, and make a Christian witness in the world.

TRANSFORMATION

Another way to talk about the emphasis on spiritual life and practice is to lift up the value of transformation. *Companions* seeks to engage people in ways that will transform both them as individuals and the church as a

---

1. "God-speech" is Ben Campbell Johnson's term for "candid, spontaneous, natural conversation about the presence and activity of the Creator" (*Speaking of God*, 11).

whole. It begins with a design that promises newcomers an opportunity to grow in faith and discipleship, no matter what their starting point. It works by inviting active members to become conversation partners with them—which invariably means the members' faith gets stretched as well, often in learning authentic ways to talk about their relationship with God. It leads two companions through an ordered set of conversations about the faith, using reflection questions that invite personal growth as well as sharing, and building on core spiritual practices that they engage in together. It invites other church members to participate by supporting these companions with their prayers. And in the process, the faith of the whole church is enlarged and strengthened, because a widening network of faith conversations and prayers are occurring all across the congregation on an ongoing basis.

Referring to the numerous churches that the apostle Paul started throughout Asia Minor, the Book of Acts says, "*So the churches were strengthened in the faith and increased in numbers daily*" (Acts 16:5). The link between spiritual growth and numerical growth that is so clear in the New Testament often frustrates twenty-first-century North American churches that have been facing chronic numerical decline for half a century. But instead of seeing just an either/or equation (as in, *we can be growing in spirit, even if we're not growing in numbers*), it would help us to consider the connection this way: while spiritually growing churches don't always have the opportunity to grow numerically as well, churches that aren't growing spiritually rarely grow in number, even when abundant opportunity lies right at their doorstep. That's because the gospel becomes most contagious when it is embodied in transformed lives, passionate faith, energized servants of God, and spiritually growing people.

Instead of just dispensing denominational or congregational *information*, *Companions* aims to invite people into mutually *transform*ing relationships, in which the Spirit of God may be continually working on us and in us and through us, and through which the church itself may be transformed and renewed for God's ever-new work in the world. As Paul writes to the Romans: "*Do not be conformed to this world, but be transformed by the renewing of your minds, so that you may discern what is the will of God— what is good and acceptable and perfect*" (Romans 12:2).

DISCERNMENT

The work of discernment, to which Paul refers above, is another important value. *Companions* reframes our consumer culture's assumptions about "church shopping," in which choosing the right product is paramount. Instead, these materials embrace the New Testament conviction that the very Spirit of the living God is at work in calling people into communities of faith and various forms of Christian service. In fact that Spirit, in order to keep us alive and growing in the faith, is forever inviting us into new experiences, new relationships, and new ministries at different seasons in our lives. Whatever the dynamics are that prompt someone to seek out a new community of faith, the gift of a companion who can be a discernment partner is an appropriate and often deeply helpful gift. It's a gift the church can offer the newcomers in their midst, regularly and generously, frequently with profound results.

In claiming discernment as a core value, *Companions* affirms that the outcome of a newcomer's participation cannot be presumed from the start. Rather the process offers a way for those not yet clear about church membership to simply explore God's love and call in their lives. This is one of the significant places where *Companions* differs from the new member class or other procedures for "joining the church." In the end, the door has to be fully open for a newcomer to say either *yes* or *no*. *Yes, this is the church for me. Yes, God is giving me a place to belong. Yes, there are ministries here I'm being called to. No, this is not the church that needs my gifts. No, this is not a community I can be fully part of. No, this is not the right time to make this commitment. Companions* starts from the conviction that if we help people discern where God is calling them, then whether or not they "join our church," we have served them rightly and well.

In addition to other less formal ways in which spiritual companions may serve as discernment partners, the resource commends participation in a *Lectio Divina* group. While this will not be possible in every congregation, it is singled out here, not just because engaging Scripture with others is a good *study* discipline, but more importantly because the ancient practice of *Lectio Divina* teaches tools for *discernment*. It trains us to listen, in Scripture, for a genuine word from God—a personal word, addressed to our own particular time and place and need. This way of reading Scripture and praying becomes especially helpful as newcomers address significant questions they need to faithfully discern, like: *What is God up to in my life here and now? Is this the congregation where I belong? Where is Jesus nudging me to take a next step in faith? What form of Christian service is the Holy Spirit inviting me to explore at this time?*

Rather than a prescribed set of steps visitors must take in order to join the church, *Companions* is a dynamic process that helps newcomers discern where God is calling them to belong and to serve.

COMMUNITY

Perhaps the most radical of the values embodied in *Companions* is the understanding that making disciples is the work of the whole church. It's not just the pastor's job or the evangelism team's responsibility; it's not the function of programs or curriculum materials to make disciples for Jesus. It's our work—work we do together as a Christian community, both by the overall patterns of our common worship and mission and by the character of our relationships with one another.

Disciple-making is the community's work because passing on the faith to those who will come after us is a primary missional challenge for the church in every age: "*Go therefore, and make disciples . . .*," Jesus said (Matthew 28:19). While we can confess from hindsight that the church may have been overly zealous in pursuit of that mission in certain periods of its history, that fact does not excuse today's disciples from seeking to fulfill, often in new ways for new times, this core commission of the risen Christ. Making and growing strong disciples of Jesus is not an optional activity: it is a missional priority that every part of the church across the theological spectrum needs to engage with integrity. Disciple-making is also the community's work because, while faith must at some point be embraced by each individual follower, it is never formed in a vacuum. Instead it must be nurtured and supported, called forth and opened up, celebrated and marked, in the company of a faithful community of believers. Like the old African proverb, "It takes a village to raise a child," so in the life of faith it takes a Christian community to make a Christian; it takes the whole congregation to grow a church.

Companions embodies this communal value first of all as a lay ministry. While pastors have an important role to play, it is primarily a supportive one. The conversations that are the core of the companioning process are nothing more (and nothing less!) than ordinary disciples sharing with one another their beliefs and their doubts, their gifts and their struggles, their experiences, their understandings, and their practices of the faith.

One might recall D. T. Niles' famous description of Christianity as "one beggar telling another where to find bread." *Companions* provides a means by which the church as a community may embody a ministry of hospitality towards those who come new to their doors.

Sunday worship, the weekly event that gathers the whole community, also has a key role to play in *Companions*. Worship attendance is emphasized as a core spiritual practice, and newcomers and their member companions are encouraged to sit together in church. A moment of public recognition occurs in worship as each new companioning relationship is begun. This gives visibility to the disciple-making work of the church. It also has the practical effect of officially introducing the congregation to newcomers in their midst who are seriously exploring a deeper connection to Christ and his church. Church members are invited to get to know these new friends, and over the eight weeks of structured conversations are regularly reminded to keep them and their member companions in prayer. When later some of these newcomers join the church, the community is eager to embrace them, because many have already been praying for them and doing their part to encourage them, and have even begun to know and love them.

BAPTISM

Finally, *Companions* is "baptismal" at its core. For some it will lead to the sacrament of baptism and a first welcome into the body of Christ. For others, it will lead to reaffirmation of an earlier baptism, as they are embraced and made part of a new Christian community. In either case, baptismal identity is at the center of what it means to be united with a Christian church.

Baptism is also at the center of what it means to live a Christian life. In Romans, Paul uses baptism as a metaphor for the life of discipleship: "*We have been buried with Christ by baptism into death, so that just as Christ was raised from the dead by the glory of the Father, so we too might walk in newness of life*" (Romans 6:4). Christian baptism is not just the single ritual moment when we are washed in the water and joined to Christ and his church. It is also the lifelong baptismal vocation that ensues from that event, the "walk" in new life, the Christian calling to love God and neighbor more and more, every day of our lives. Whether we are committed believers when we are baptized, or tiny babes in arms, God begins something with us then that continues throughout our earthly lives. We live our baptism day by day and year by year until finally, as the ancient funeral prayer affirms, that baptism is "complete in death."[2]

Companions embraces this understanding of baptismal vocation, and seeks to support it by encouraging a lifetime of spiritual maturation. Exploring our relationship with God in conversation with another is good nourishment for that journey, for any follower of Jesus. Those new to the church and its faith have things to learn from long-time disciples and church members. Likewise, long-time disciples and church members have things to learn from those who come new to the church and its faith. And all of us always have more faith and hope and love to grow into, more of God in Jesus Christ to come to know, and new avenues for Christian service in the world to explore. The liturgies at the beginning and end of the *Companions* process are designed to be conducted at the font, open and filled with water, in order to make visible for all the church the baptismal roots of Christian living.

Those familiar with the ancient catechumenate of the first five Christian centuries will recognize that virtually all of the values identified here are informed by those earliest patterns—the invitation into baptismal living, the emphasis on practicing the faith, the apprenticeship or mentoring model, the involvement of the whole community, the focus on the spiritual life, prayer and discernment. *Companions* is not a full-blown contemporary adaptation of the catechumenate, nor does it strive to be. Others (Roman Catholics, Episcopalians, and Lutherans, along with a handful of Presbyterians and Methodists) are doing that well and with good result. But *Companions* does aim to help regular mainline, evangelical, and independent Protestant congregations draw on the spiritual values of the catechumenate in order to move away from the information-based models for new member ministry that in so many churches have become tired and spiritually bankrupt, and to move instead towards discernment-based patterns for making and growing disciples[3]—patterns that promise to be spiritually life-giving, both for those who visit our congregations and for the church itself.

---

2. *Book of Common Worship*, 921.

3. For first suggesting the language to distinguish between "information-based" and "discernment-based" new member processes, I am indebted to the Rev. Bart Roush, who visited Trinity Presbyterian Church in 2011 conducting research for his doctoral thesis. See Roush, "Incorporating Adults," 111, 122, 149, 165–67.

3

The Conversations

THE EIGHT CONVERSATIONS ARE designed to follow an ordered sequence, with flexibility (for scheduling's sake) regarding the placement of the two group gatherings on Scripture and Christian belief. As a normative order, I have placed Scripture in the third week and belief in the sixth, but when necessary these two may be scheduled at other midway points that are convenient for all participants.

1. Vocation: The Rhythms of Living
2. Prayer: A Way of Knowing God

A. *Scripture: The Story and Our Stories*

3. Forgiveness: A Way of Loving Neighbors
4. Gratitude: A Way of Living with Things

B. *Belief: Who Is This Jesus?*

5. Community: Belonging to One Another
6. Calling: Sent to Serve the World

At this point, the reader will want to refer to the conversation guides themselves, in order to make the most sense of the descriptions that follow. These may be found in chapter 5, on "The Materials."

1. VOCATION: THE RHYTHMS OF LIVING

The first conversation is about vocation, understood broadly to mean who we are and what we do with our lives. In this sense, vocation includes marriage and family, volunteering and personal pursuits, as well as the activities of the workplace. What we do in the world and in the home, who loves us and who we belong to in this life—all are fundamental ways we are known to one another. This initial *Companions* conversation is designed to give two new acquaintances a natural and easy opportunity to start getting to know each other by sharing about work and family, leisure and rest. At the same time, the conversation is framed by a story about Jesus seeking solitude in the wilderness, and the larger biblical context of sabbath with its spiritual rhythms of work and rest. At the end, the prayer commends several verses from Psalms 42 and 63, which express our longing for God in the midst of our daily lives.

The next three numbered topics—Prayer, Forgiveness, and Gratitude—prompt companions to explore our primary relationships: relationship with God, relationships with our neighbors, and relationships with the material world in which we live.

2. PRAYER: A WAY OF KNOWING GOD

"A Way of Knowing God" focuses on the development of a life of prayer. While we will encounter God in many places outside our conscious prayers—like in the beauty of a sunset or the vastness of the ocean, like in the sacred joy of loving and being loved, like seeing Jesus in the faces lined up at the local soup kitchen, like being awed by sublime music or creative art—still the practice of prayer is key to nurturing a lifelong friendship with the triune God. It is the regular habit of speaking and listening to God that allows us to integrate all our experiences of the holy into this one central and dynamic relationship. The Scripture text, the apostle Paul's advice to the Philippians about thanksgiving and intercession, provides a helpful starting place for an honest conversation about our prayer lives—where we're satisfied and where we long to grow. For this conversation, the concluding prayer is the Lord's Prayer, the one Jesus himself gave us.

3. FORGIVENESS: A WAY OF LOVING NEIGHBORS

"A Way of Loving Neighbors" invites reflection on how we interact with other people—our friends and family, colleagues, our communities, the world of nations—all those whom Scripture would call our "neighbors." Here, the topic of forgiveness is central to considering how human relationships are sustained, deepened, transformed—and when badly broken, redeemed—by God's forgiveness and one another's. Jesus' instructions from Matthew's Gospel on what to do when we've been wronged form the backdrop for this conversation. Companions are encouraged to reflect on those relationships where some offense occurred and forgiveness was needed—where we were the offended, or where we were the offender; where forgiveness was given, or where it was withheld. There are also opportunities to recall those relationships that are untroubled, to ponder what keeps them strong and life-giving, and to share personal experiences of God's forgiveness. For Jesus, loving God and loving neighbors are the two commandments that summarize the whole law: it's important that we keep them both front and center in our lives of faith.

4. GRATITUDE: A WAY OF LIVING WITH THINGS

"A Way of Living with Things" turns to our relationships with the material world—our possessions, our money, the land and skies and earth's other creatures, God's whole creation—with a focus on gratitude as essential to faithful living. The Scripture passage is Paul's encouragement to the Corinthians to give joyfully; in just a few words, it eloquently makes the connection between grace, gratitude, and generosity. The sharing questions prompt a conversation that might go in any of several directions, but always anchored in the conviction that generosity is born of gratitude, and gratitude comes from acknowledging all the gifts we have been given by the grace of a loving God. Companions might talk together about money and how they use it; about possessions and the way they can "own" us; about their sense of Christian stewardship; about how giving can become, beyond obligation, a true joy; about the habits of gratitude we cultivate, and plenty more. As followers, it matters that we live with our world and our things in ways that express our faith. The prayers for this week focus on all the things for which we are grateful.

The two conversations on Scripture and Christian belief are designed to take place in the context of a larger group dialogue. These two group gatherings will include the church's pastor and any other pairs of companions currently working through the series of eight conversations. If desired, an open invitation could be extended to interested church members as well. The group context allows for wider dialogue about the theological core of the faith, for cultivation of friendships among current church newcomers, and for the establishment of a pastoral relationship between each of those newcomers and the pastor. Scripture and belief were chosen as the topics for the group gatherings because they are two areas where the pastor's theological training may be put to good use. While each of the group conversations will include components of presentation and discussion, the related conversation guides are still intended for one-on-one dialogue in companion pairs during portions of these two gatherings.

(A) SCRIPTURE: THE STORY AND OUR STORIES

The first group conversation on Scripture links prayer and reading Scripture as the two core spiritual practices that are needed to support a Christian life. The conversation guide on "The Story and Our Stories" invites companions to examine together how much of the Bible they have read, which parts of it they know best and which they'd like to know better, how often they turn to it and for what purposes. A passage from Deuteronomy spells out some of the very tangible ways the ancient Hebrews kept God's Word close at hand and ready to act on, inviting reflection on the ways we keep the words of Scripture near and available for use in our daily living. A more imaginative question echoes the discussion from the overall group gathering theme on "The Bible as One Story": "If you were to describe the Bible as one long story," it asks, "what would the title be? How about some of the chapter headings?" At the end, the prayer borrows a few verses from Psalm 19, an ancient song about the joy of keeping God's commandments.

(B) BELIEF: WHO IS THIS JESUS?

The second group conversation on Christian belief leaves room for asking theological questions, while stretching companions to articulate to one another what they *can* claim about their relationship with Jesus Christ. Since the person and work of Jesus are pivotal to Christian faith, the Scripture passage that launches this conversation is Luke's record of Jesus' famous question to his disciples: "*Who do you say that I am?*" (Luke 9:20). The sharing questions invite reflection both about who Jesus is and about what he has done for us—what difference his life and death make. Companions are encouraged to share both their convictions about Jesus and their questions, doubts, struggles, wonderings. In the context of group explorations into "What We Believe," participants are encouraged to raise "everything they ever wanted to know about the faith, but were afraid to ask!" The suggested prayer for this meeting is a biblical prayer from Ephesians 1, which asks God to help us come to know Jesus more fully.

#5 COMMUNITY: BELONGING TO ONE ANOTHER

The week on community provides a chance to get concrete about the varied ministries of the congregation, and to reflect on the importance of being surrounded by a community of faith. The apostle Paul's famous analogy from 1 Corinthians, likening the church to a human body, reminds us that "Belonging to One Another" in the church is not just optional; it's a core part of what it means to be Christian. Companions are invited to share how the church and church people have shaped their faith, why worship matters, and what kinds of church experiences have been most satisfying for them. Here also is an opportunity for member companions to inform newcomers about the particular ministries of the congregation, and to encourage their involvement in service ministries, discipleship opportunities, and worship experiences that can keep them growing. This week, companions are encouraged to lift up together their prayers for the church.

#6 CALLING: SENT TO SERVE THE WORLD

The final conversation on calling presses towards thoughtful discernment regarding the questions of baptismal faith, church membership, and Christ's call to service in the world. For newcomers who have been considering uniting with the church, this is an opportunity to talk with their member companions about this decision. The scriptural context for the conversation is Jesus' appointment of the Twelve, calling them together as disciples to be with him, and sending them out as apostles to serve the world. For us too, discerning where we are called to be *with Jesus* in his church, and where we are *sent out* to serve him in the world, is important spiritual work that we can help each other do prayerfully and well. "Sent to Serve the World" brings the eight conversations full circle, with Frederich Buechner's telling definition of our God-given vocation as that place "where our deep gladness and the world's deep hunger meet."[4] For this final conversation, the prayer is the *Companions* daily prayer from Ephesians 3.

The sequence of *Companions* conversations has an order to it that builds from simple friendship to shared discernment. In between are numerous invitations to explore what a life dedicated to loving God and neighbor looks like, and to share with a fellow seeker our various efforts, both successful and failed, to sustain that life. The conversations go back and forth between exploring what we believe and examining how we practice those beliefs. Week by week they offer opportunity not just to talk about the life of discipleship, but to engage in it together, through shared reading of Scripture, and prayer for and with one another. All along the way, there is simple friendship, spiritual support, opportunities to develop trust and offer freedom, and always the possibility, where mutually desired, for going deeper.

---

4. Buechner, *Wishful Thinking*, 95.

4

The Methods

THIS SECTION ADDRESSES PRACTICAL matters of implementation, adaptation, and leadership for *Companions* as it is integrated into a congregation's life and ministry.

CONVERSATION

Business consultant Margaret Wheatley is convinced about the power of conversation. "I believe we can change the world if we start listening to one another again," she writes, "simple, honest, human conversation . . . where we each have a chance to speak, we each feel heard, and we each listen well."[5] "Conversation," she insists further, "is the natural way humans think together."[6] If *Companions* could be said to have an educational methodology, it would be conversation, because that is what's at the heart of it—not lectures or presentations, not group discussion or debate or recitation or role play—just simple, one-on-one, human conversation.

Companions provides an open-ended conversation guide to help prompt each of the eight conversations about Christian faith and discipleship. These one-page guides all start with Scripture, pose reflection questions for sharing, and conclude with prayer: Word–Share–Prayer. The Word–Share–Prayer format was developed by preeminent church leader and author E. Stanley Ott, of the Vital Churches Institute, as a Bible study

---

5. Wheatley, *Turning to One Another*, 3.
6. Ibid., 29.

process for groups, teams, committees, and boards (see the bibliography for a reference to one of his books). Since its introduction, literally thousands of church leaders in many denominations have found Word–Share–Prayer to be an extremely useful and versatile tool for engaging people of faith with Scripture, with God, and with each other. It has been adapted here, with the author's permission, as the format for the *Companions* conversations.

Companions uses conversation as the primary vehicle for two people to develop a spiritual friendship. The one-page Word–Share–Prayer sheets that serve as guides for the eight faith conversations can be found in chapter 5, on "The Materials." A passage of Scripture relevant to the topic is printed for reading and reflection. Questions for exploring both text and topic suggest several directions a conversation might take as personal experiences are recalled and shared. And companions are invited to pray together, claiming God's presence in their friendship, and lifting up special challenges or joys their conversation has brought to light.

Word–Share–Prayer works best if each partner has read the Scripture passage and thought about the reflection questions *before* they start sharing their responses. This can be accomplished very simply by spending the first five to ten minutes of their time together in silence: each one may read the text, ponder the questions, and jot down responses that come to mind. Alternately, the two could agree to do this ahead of time, as "homework" for their conversation. In that case, it will be useful to reread the passage of Scripture, perhaps aloud, when they come together so that the hearing of it is fresh. While it's always tempting, in our verbal, extroverted culture, to jump straight into the talking and sharing . . . *taking time first for personal reflection* embodies several important values. It insists that each person's experience is important and worthy of sharing. It helps insure that the introverts aren't so easily silenced by the extroverts. And it says that time to think deeply is honored and thoughtfulness encouraged.

The questions in the "Share" section always include at least one that is related to the Scripture passage, and others that suggest different directions a good conversation on the topic might take. For example, the Word–Share–Prayer guide on gratitude could lead to a conversation about how we live gratefully, or about our attitudes towards money and material possessions, or about our patterns of giving and generosity, or about our stewardship of the earth and all of life. Companions need to understand that the printed questions are suggestions, and that they are free to focus their conversation in whatever direction is most fruitful for them. It's not as

The Methods

important to cover everything on the list as it is to share openly with each other around those questions that are the most personally compelling.

Prayer together at the conclusion of each conversation is an integral part of the *Companions* design. While some people will be more comfortable with this than others, prayer is not an optional activity here—something that can be skipped if time runs out, or conveniently forgotten if neither partner can muster the courage to begin. The Word–Share–Prayer guides are written to make this act of praying together simple, accessible, and increasingly comfortable with practice. In some weeks, a specific prayer is suggested for praying aloud, by one voice or both together. The *Companions* daily prayer card, based on Ephesians 3, may always be used instead or when there is no printed prayer. And if each person can name just one or two specific needs he or she has for prayer that week, then each partner's job in praying for the other is made simple. Companions may be encouraged to experiment, try different things, talk about what felt awkward or genuine, what helped or hindered . . . but never to just overlook the prayers. They are an important way we may grow, and grow together, in Christ.

Stan Ott's Word–Share–Prayer format takes the two core Christian disciplines of prayer and Scripture, and combines them in a simple, self-directed conversational process. *Companions* sets up a sequence of Word–Share–Prayer conversation topics that can help two strangers become friends in the faith. At each step along the way, there are opportunities for going deeper in friendship and in love of God and neighbor, and there is freedom individually and together to choose what will work best toward that end.

PRAYER

Prayer is both essential to the Christian life and integral to the design of this resource. In a variety of different ways, *Companions* seeks to enable and strengthen the practice of a life of prayer for all participants—newcomers, member companions, and congregations.

Prayer in a relationship with God is equivalent to conversation in a close friendship. It's what allows the relationship to grow and develop. Prayer is the way we spend quality time with God, on a regular basis, nurturing that divine relationship just as we would nurture any other friendship. And like ordinary conversation, praying involves both speaking and listening—speaking our hearts to God, and learning to listen for what God is saying to us. When we pray, sometimes we express gratitude for everything we've been given. Sometimes we ask for help on behalf of others. Sometimes we dare to admit what we most need from God for ourselves. Sometimes we pray for the life of the world. Sometimes we search the Scriptures for an encouraging word from God. Sometimes we just sit quietly in God's presence. Sometimes we sing or offer praise for who God is and how amazing it is that God loves us. In the end, the richest fruits of a life of prayer are not that our particular petitions are granted, but that we come to know and love God more and more deeply as our truest Friend.

In *Companions*, the daily prayer card, based on the apostle Paul's prayer for Christian friends in Ephesus, is an invitation for two people to pray daily for one another. This is not a prayer for any specific tangible need—concrete intercessions can be added as personal needs are shared—but a broad, generous prayer for a partner's inner well-being, for their growth in grace and in the love of Christ. Who among us would not be encouraged to have such a prayer prayed for us, day after day, by a faithful friend?! If some prefer to use a different prayer or pray in their own words, that's perfectly fine. But Ephesians 3 offers an easy place to start (or maybe a place to fall back to) on the adventure of becoming spiritual friends and partners in prayer.

The conversation guides, all of which conclude with prayer, insist that it's not enough for two people to talk with each other, that God is an essential third party in any spiritual friendship. The invitation for companions to pray together, each time they meet, acknowledges the Spirit's constant presence with them, and helps them invite God into their conversation and their relationship. Praying together will stretch both companions, some of whom may be unaccustomed to praying aloud, to pray not only *for* each other, but also *with* each other.

Praying in our own words is regularly encouraged in this resource. God doesn't need fancy words, just honest ones, and speaking simply and directly to God can help us get clear about what is in our own hearts. At the same time, a number of biblical prayers, including the psalms, are commended. These ancient prayers unite us to our ancestors in the faith and to the Scriptures. They loan us their words when our own are not enough. And although they are centuries old, these prayers may become ours as we pray them. The materials within this resource make use of biblical prayers from Ephesians 1, Ephesians 3, Matthew 6/Luke 11, along with Psalms 19, 42, 63, 100, and 139.

The prayers of the congregation for newcomers and their companions are also important. A simple reminder in the weekly bulletin/newsletter/website can help members of the church participate through prayer in supporting the new friends in their midst. And if prayer leads to action, as it surely should, then their prayers will soon become small acts of hospitality and friendship extended in the Spirit of Christ. In this simple way, through prayer, the outsiders God sends among us are encouraged and supported, and the whole congregation is given concrete work to do in building up the church.

We all know that even lifelong Christians sometimes struggle to integrate prayer into their daily living, and that every follower of Jesus has room to grow in a life of prayer. The practices of prayer that are built into *Companions* are intended to help anyone establish, renew, or deepen that ongoing conversation with God that can sustain them for a lifetime.

MEMBER COMPANIONS: GETTING STARTED

The first challenge will be to gather a group of people who are willing to serve as member companions. Look for members who are active in the life of the church, and regular participants in its worship. Look for people whose faith matters to them—not that they have all the answers figured out, but that they've wrestled with some of the questions. Look for people who seek to actively live their faith—by the values they claim and by the spiritual practices they endeavor to build into their lives.

In addition, seek out those individuals who have gifts for hospitality—not in the sense of being good at entertaining, but in the sense of making others feel comfortable and welcome in their presence. A genuine interest in people is part of this. An ability to listen is key. So is the capacity to draw others into conversation. This means there are both introverts and extroverts who will make great companions. Gifts for spiritual hospitality will also suggest those who are able, or at least willing to try, to speak about their faith and articulate some of the ways they have come to know God in Jesus Christ. Hospitable people are generally comfortable with themselves, and approach others with a profound and generous respect.

In recruiting member companions, it will be important initially to invite individuals whom you believe have the needed gifts, rather than to ask for volunteers. This avoids the awkwardness of having to turn down a volunteer who may be well-intentioned but not well-suited for such a ministry. Among those serving, it's good to have people of both genders, and a mix of ages. Married couples willing to serve together as companions for a newcomer couple are also helpful.

The number of companions needed to begin will depend on the average number of visitors/newcomers participating in the church at any given time. It's good to have an initial pool of member companions trained and ready—enough to provide the best chance of a "good match" for each interested newcomer, but not so many that those trained have to wait more than a few months for a first assignment. Remember that not all the member companions will be needed at once, and that there will likely be breaks between companioning assignments. Assignments will generally last eight to twelve weeks, depending on how quickly the two companions proceed through the sequence of conversations.

And here's an added bonus: once *Companions* has become part of the congregation's life, a great source of additional member companions is the church's newest members. Having experienced the companioning conversations for themselves as newcomers, they can step up to being companions for others with good confidence, enthusiasm, and a minimum of training.

The outline of a training session for member companions is included in the appendix. It will need to be modified to fit the particular dynamics in each congregational setting, but it provides a sense of the basics that need to be covered, and the values that need to be emphasized, in order to adequately equip volunteer member companions for this ministry.

NEWCOMERS: MATCHING AND ENCOURAGING

Matching up each newcomer with an appropriate member companion requires some thoughtfulness. It's important to find a match that will give both persons, and especially the newcomer, a positive experience and a good chance to make a real friend in the church. It may be helpful to identify a common interest or two—hobbies, kids or no kids, geographical connections, similar vocation, etc. On the other hand, someone who works in the same office, or is already a good friend, is probably too familiar to be the best choice for this purpose. Personalities factor in too. You might need an easy conversationalist to help draw out a particularly shy visitor, or someone who can talk theology for a newcomer with strong intellectual interests.

Newcomers who are single should normally be paired up with a companion of the same gender; there are exceptions to this rule, but it generally helps avoid awkwardness. Age is a factor too, although not always in the same way. People naturally look for friends in their own age group first, so peers can be a good match. But just as often, a grandmother will make a terrific companion for a young single woman, or a young man will be the perfect partner to engage a recent widower, and a mature couple can become great mentors for some newly-marrieds.

While it's possible to assign just one member companion to work with a newcomer couple, it's not ideal. Try instead to pair the new couple with a member couple, or with two companions. This can help ensure that both newcomer spouses get fully engaged. It also gives the four companions some options: they can decide to meet together as a foursome or to split up into pairs for some or all of the conversations.

Having someone who will check in with the newcomers and with their member companions every few weeks is important. This can be done by the pastor or by a church member who serves as a coordinator. A quick "How's it going?" at church or a phone call during the week is enough to let people know they haven't been forgotten, and that somebody cares how they're getting along. It allows any concerns that may arise to be addressed before they become problematic. It can help a pair that's gotten bogged down or unduly delayed to get refocused. And it helps church leaders anticipate when companions are coming to the end of their conversations, and which newcomers may soon be ready to request church membership.

LECTIO DIVINA

Much has been written on *Lectio Divina*, or holy reading, in recent decades. So for those who may be unfamiliar with this ancient practice, I happily encourage you to consult other sources. Two excellent places to start are: *SoulFeast,* by Marjorie Thompson, and *Eat This Book,* by Eugene Peterson (see the bibliography for complete reference information).

Broadly speaking, *Lectio Divina* is a way of reading Scripture that encourages listening and discernment, as distinct from study and discussion. While biblical scholarship and study certainly have their place in Christian life, a prayerful approach to Scripture has different and unique gifts to offer. We could say generally that if the purpose of Bible study is to help us learn *about* God and Jesus and the Scriptures, the purpose of *Lectio Divina* is to read the Scriptures as a means for entering into dialogue *with* God. To say it another way, *Lectio Divina* is a practice that helps people pay attention to their lives and to where God may be at work in them.

A simple process for leading group *Lectio Divina* is outlined in the appendix. It follows the ancient pattern of a four-part movement from reading (*lectio*), to reflecting (*meditatio*), to responding (*oratio*), to rest (*contemplatio*). There is nothing original about the outline. It has been borrowed from many places and honed with the help of *Lectio Divina* group participants in congregations I have served. Other writers on the spiritual life have compiled similar outlines, with their own personal touches, which you may find more helpful. Along with the outline, you will find the template for a bookmark. This can be a useful tool to help participants stay focused, learn the rhythms of *Lectio Divina*, and even incorporate it into their own devotional reading at home if they wish.

While *Lectio Divina* is not essential to the design of *Companions*, it can provide a helpful complement. By offering practice in listening for God's voice, *Lectio Divina* invites renewal in the spiritual life, and supports newcomers in the discernment work that exploring faith and seeking a church home generally entails. Newcomers in any congregation's life will quite naturally be asking themselves questions like: *Is this the church for me? Can I find a place to belong here? Can this community help me grow spiritually? Am I ready to seek baptism, or renew the faith in which I was once baptized? Where is God inviting me to serve? Are there ministries here I am drawn to become part of? Shall I join this congregation? or participate without joining? Should I look for a different church instead?* These kinds of questions are matters for spiritual discernment—listening to one's life in order to "hear" where God may be leading. And the practice of *Lectio Divina* offers tools for this discernment work that can be deeply helpful.

It must be acknowledged, however, that offering a weekly *Lectio Divina* group will not be possible in every congregation. *Companions* has been designed so that this component, while valuable and encouraged, is not essential. If yours is one of those congregations, do not be deterred from participating fully in *Companions* in all other regards.

On the other hand, if your congregation might be interested in starting a *Lectio Divina* group, this need not be a difficult or complicated undertaking. An easy way to begin is to offer *Lectio Divina* each week on one of the passages of Scripture that will be read in worship on Sunday. This works especially well when the group is open to the whole congregation,

THE METHODS

not just *Companions* participants. Use the outline provided in the appendix or consult with other resources as you choose. With a little practice, any person of committed faith can lead a group in this simple four-part reflection process, and help people listen for God's living and lively Word in their lives. (If the pastor is the leader, she or he should take care that the sermon for the day not become the focus of the group's reflection.) Using the texts for Sunday as a starting place has the added benefit of inviting participants into a deeper engagement with the church's worship—that place where God regularly speaks to our communal life in the liturgy of Word and sacrament.

FLEXIBILITY AND ADAPTATION

It should be clear by now that *Companions* is adaptable to a wide variety of people and churches. Because it uses a companioning model rather than a programmatic one, there is freedom for each pair of companions to choose when and where they meet, as well as how rapidly they proceed through the eight conversations. Even the "content" of their exploration together is flexible—shaped by which questions they spend their time on, what they choose to share of themselves, and how overall they relate to one another.

The possibilities for getting together are wide open. Meeting places might include each other's homes, a restaurant or coffee shop, a park, a quiet corner at the office, a room at the church. It is best to look for someplace where they won't be distracted or interrupted. Meeting times might be midweek or weekend, before or after work, on a lunch break, during children's naptime, or they might be tied to church programs, like after worship or before choir rehearsal. Sharing a meal, even occasionally, or meeting for coffee provides the added dimension of some table fellowship, which can be a plus. It's best, if possible, to find a regular weekly time and place to meet, and then adjust if conflicts arise. Companions who meet weekly can complete the conversations in eight weeks, or they may decide to skip some weeks in order to accommodate holidays, travel plans, illness, or personal schedules. Doubling up on two conversations in one meeting is not advisable. If an occasional pair of companions moves extra slowly, adjustments can always be made to invite them to a later group gathering.

In addition, there is flexibility for the congregations that use *Companions*. Smaller congregations, or those with few visitors, can support a fluid schedule, with newcomers and member companions beginning, one pair at a time, whenever they are ready. This means that at any given time the church might have just one pair or half a dozen pairs of companions, each at a different place in the sequence of the eight conversations. In this case, the two group gatherings are set to best coordinate with their various schedules. Some of those pairs might even find themselves attending the "second" group gathering first, and the "first" one second (not a problem)! And if a congregation has only one active pair of companions at a time, the pastor can simply join them for the two conversations about Scripture and Christian belief, which in that case become a slightly more intimate "group" gathering of three.

On the other hand, larger churches, or those with a steady influx of first-time visitors, may opt for an annual *Companions* schedule, with publicized start dates towards which newcomers may be directed. Depending on the need, there could be one to four cycles of *Companions* in a calendar year. Each cycle would include a Sunday on which newcomers and their member companions are paired up, introduced to the congregation, and given their conversation packets; an eight-to-twelve-week period during which they would meet together for those conversations; two group gatherings, scheduled during the same eight to twelve weeks, for conversations with other companion pairs and the church's pastor; and then a Sunday when those who choose to join the church reaffirm their baptismal identity and are received into membership. That final Sunday needs to be scheduled so as to allow adequate time for all the pairs to complete their conversations and, where applicable, for church leaders to meet with those newcomers seeking membership in the congregation. A minimum of three months should be allowed to complete a cycle.

In especially large and fast-growing congregations, overlapping cycles could be scheduled to accommodate more than four groups in a given year. Alternately, if more than six to eight pairs of companions are active simultaneously, two sets of group gatherings could be scheduled during that cycle, so that the groups don't become too large for good participation.

Another opportunity for fruitful adaptation is with some creative use of the Word–Share–Prayer sheets themselves. While the sequence of eight conversations is designed to help newcomers find a place among a community of God's people, they can also be used in other settings and for broader purposes. Imagine church members being invited to pair up as prayer partners and commit to working through the conversations for their own enjoyment and spiritual growth. Perhaps this could be a Lenten or Eastertide discipline. Or what if persons of differing theological perspectives

THE METHODS

were intentionally paired together to do this? Here the conversations would serve a reconciliation or peace-making purpose. Imagine using any one of the conversation guides as a thirty-minute spiritual sharing exercise at the start of a church committee or council meeting. Or imagine holding a congregational faith-sharing event in which people were invited to pair up and engage in one of the conversations. What about using the conversations at a leadership retreat, for team building and practice in sharing the faith? There are lots of possibilities that could all help strengthen the church's fellowship, nurture the capacity for thoughtful "God-speech"[7] among God's people, and contribute to spiritually alive churches and growing, practicing disciples.

PASTORAL AND OTHER LEADERSHIP

The role of the pastor in *Companions* is an important one. While member companions are the ones who have most of the direct contact with participating newcomers, the pastor often has the first and most obvious access to church visitors. She or he is in a position to help direct visitors towards participation in *Companions*. And throughout the process, the pastor has an indirect supportive role to play with both newcomers and member companions. In multiple-staff churches, it may make sense for an associate pastor with responsibilities for outreach/evangelism or spiritual nurture to take on these functions.

In addition to pastoral support and encouragement, *Companions* is designed with the expectation that a pastor will participate in three specific events: the training of member companions, and the two group gatherings with the companion pairs. Training would not likely be any more frequent than annually, and the pastor's leadership here provides an opportunity to shape this ministry, as well as to support and encourage its volunteers. The group gatherings would reoccur with each new group of companions. The pastor may lead these gatherings, or share the leadership with others in the church, but regardless of who leads, these are great opportunities for a pastor to get acquainted and establish an initial pastoral relationship with the newest folks in the church.

For *Companions* to work well, someone needs to take on a handful of coordinating and communication tasks. This *Companions* coordinator can

---

7. "God-speech" is Ben Campbell Johnson's term for "candid, spontaneous, natural conversation about the presence and activity of the Creator" (*Speaking of God*, 11).

be the pastor, or another church leader. A decision about the coordinator function might be made based on the pastor's interest and availability, on the number of people involved in *Companions* at any given time, on the emergence of a suitably gifted lay leader, or on other factors. Or the necessary functions might be divided up between a pastor and a church member serving as coordinator.

Regardless of who takes on the coordinating roles, the following are the primary tasks that will need to be attended to:

- recruiting member companions
- scheduling training sessions for member *Companions* as needed
- training member companions
- building relationships week by week with the church's worship visitors
- inviting newcomers to participate in *Companions*
- matching interested newcomers with member companions
- setting dates for introducing new companion pairs in worship
- preparing packets of the *Companions* materials and distributing them to participants
- checking in every few weeks with newcomers and their companions to see how things are going
- troubleshooting any problems that arise
- scheduling the group gatherings
- leading the group gatherings
- communicating with church leaders about newcomers ready to join the church
- coordinating dates for baptism and/or the receiving of new members in worship
- encouraging the whole congregation to participate through prayer and support
- generating ongoing publicity about *Companions* opportunities
- coordinating *Companions* events with the church calendar

The Methods

These coordination and communication tasks have an administrative dimension. But they are first and foremost pastoral functions, whether the pastor fulfills them or not. By knowing all the participants and being aware of the big picture, the *Companions* coordinator has a unique opportunity to embody a spirit of hospitality and grace. He or she can help make sure each participant feels supported and valued by the church, and is helped to grow in his or her own faith and life as a follower of Jesus.

The appendix contains a variety of additional "Resources for Leaders." There are outlines for a Member Companion Training Session, for both group gatherings, and for an extra session with those newcomers who are preparing for baptism. There are suggestions for the format a church council might use in meeting with newcomers who desire to join the church. There is a simple group process for leading a *Lectio Divina* group. There are also sample letters and publicity materials. While all these will need to be adapted somewhat to each particular congregational setting and circumstances, they provide a map of many of the possibilities as well as a guide to what may be important to emphasize.

The appendix also contains two brief liturgical resources: one to use as newcomers and their member companions are paired up and introduced to the church, the other a liturgy for Renewal of Baptism for those uniting with the congregation. The latter is based on the Service for Reaffirmation of the Baptismal Covenant that is found in the 1993 *Book of Common Worship* of the Presbyterian Church (U.S.A.).[8] If the person uniting with the congregation has not been baptized, then this liturgy would be replaced with a celebration of the sacrament of baptism. Churches in other denominations will want to consult their own denominational resources for appropriate liturgical guidance. Congregations may also have local worship patterns for receiving new members that are desirable to maintain.

---

8. Presbyterian Church (U.S.A.), *Book of Common Worship*, 455–62.

5

The Materials

THESE MATERIALS ARE REPRODUCIBLE sheets that may be copied, in whatever quantity is needed, to create a packet for each participant in *Companions*. To make copies from the book, simply adjust the copier so that it enlarges each page to standard letter-size. Or to receive a PDF file with all the materials copy-ready, send an email request to: companionsresources@gmail.com.

Sets of the materials may be printed, assembled and inserted into simple pocket folders for distribution. Packets for newcomers and packets for member companions are identical, with the one exception of the Member Companions Guidelines, which should be *omitted from the newcomers' packets*.

It is encouraged to print the Word–Share–Prayer conversation guides on colored paper, to distinguish them from the other materials, which should all be on white. Print the six numbered conversation guides on one color, and the two lettered ones (for the group gatherings) on a different color. The daily prayer cards may be printed on card stock, if desired, and cut apart before inserting in the folder.

The conversation guides for group gatherings A and B should be placed last in the stack of eight conversations. Please note: there are two options for group gathering A. Place only the first one in the packet; if you decide to use the alternate instead, it may be handed out when the gathering takes place.

In the conversation guides, abbreviations identify the Scripture passages for reflection as coming from either the New Revised Standard Version (NRSV), Today's New International Version (TNIV), or Eugene Peterson's *The Message*.

Welcome to *Companions*!

A Process for Exploring Faith, Discipleship and Church Membership

THANK YOU FOR EXPRESSING an interest in exploring Christian faith and discipleship, and the possibility of membership at our church. We believe that God is doing something exciting in your life now! We hope we can help you respond to God in growing ways, as you explore this new community of faith.

As the name suggests, we offer a **companioning ministry** for newcomers to our community. You will be paired with an active church member who will befriend you, introduce you to the congregation's life and ministry, engage in a series of conversations with you, and help you pay attention to what God is doing in your life now.

Three commitments are key. You and your member companion will be asked to:

- *Pray* for each other daily.
- *Worship* together with the church on Sundays.
- *Meet together* weekly for a conversation about Christian life and faith.

To be more specific, the *Companions* exploration process includes the following components:

1. **Public welcome in worship:** You will be introduced to the congregation and welcomed as a friend who is on a journey towards baptismal renewal (or baptism) and possible church membership. The congregation will be encouraged to keep you in prayer.

2. **Weekly conversations with a companion:** You and your member companion will meet, at times and places of your own choosing, for eight conversations on such topics as vocation, prayer, forgiveness, gratitude, community, and service.

3. **Two group gatherings:** For two of those eight conversations, you and your companion will be joined by others concurrently participating in *Companions*, and by the congregation's pastor(s). These two conversations will focus on the Bible and Christian beliefs.

4. **Reading Scripture:** If the church has a *Lectio Divina* group, you and your companion will be encouraged to participate in it together. This ancient method of Bible study engages the Scriptures in a prayerful and personal way, inviting reflection and active listening for God's Word in our lives.

5. **Meeting with church leaders:** If you determine that this is the congregation where God is calling you to be in ministry and you desire to join the church, an opportunity for you to meet with the appropriate church leaders will be arranged.

6. **Uniting with the congregation** will then take place in worship, in a service of thanksgiving recalling baptism—or if you have never been baptized, the sacrament of baptism. In the latter case, you will have an opportunity to meet with the pastor in preparation for baptism.

Our hope is that this companion relationship will:

- encourage honest sharing, asking questions, talking about faith
- take seriously what God is doing in your life now
- start where you are on your spiritual journey and help you take next steps
- help you get fully integrated into the life of the church
- help you consider where God is calling you into fellowship and service
- nurture both you and your member companion to grow in faith and discipleship
- build friendships that strengthen the whole church

About Church Membership

By the time you have completed the series of conversations with your companion, you may be ready to become a member of the church, or you may have determined that God is calling you in another direction. Whatever you choose, we will remain grateful for your friendship, your trust, and any ways we may have served you on your spiritual journey. If in fact the *Companions* process has confirmed your desire to join this church, we will be ready to receive you gladly into membership and service with us.

Because the church is formed by baptism, joining a new community of faith recalls our own baptism, and receiving a new member reminds the whole church of its baptismal roots. Whether you will be transferring your membership from another congregation or returning to the church after years away, whether you will be renewing your baptismal vows or professing Christian faith for the first time, joining a church is always a baptismal occasion.

For this reason, the public welcome in worship and the reception into church membership are conducted at the baptismal font. If you have been previously baptized, you will not be baptized again, but you will be invited to remember and renew your lifelong baptismal identity and calling as a follower of Jesus, even as you promise to become an active part of this community of faith and its ministry. If you have never been baptized, your baptism is the way you join the church.

Member Companion Guidelines

THE CORE CONCEPT OF this ministry is pairing newcomers ready to explore a commitment to Christ and his church with member companions already active in church life. The basic covenant companions are asked to make to each other, for eight weeks, involves these practices:

- *Pray* for each other daily.
- *Worship* together with the church on Sundays.
- *Meet together* weekly for a conversation about Christian life and faith.

Companions: You are asked first and foremost to be a friend and companion on a journey of faith. You do not need to be "experts," imparting information or offering definitive answers. Rather, you are asked to share your own experiences in living the life of discipleship—experiences that may include both successes and failures, convictions and doubts. Your role is to encourage your exploration partners, wherever they are in their Christian journey, to take some next steps and grow in the life of faith.

Prayer: Pray for each other daily. While this may become a friendship in all the ordinary ways we treasure our friends, it is also a spiritual friendship; prayer is an essential part of it. A card in your packet contains a prayer that may provide a helpful starting place. Put it on your refrigerator or bathroom mirror or in your Bible—any place where you will see and use it regularly—and encourage your companion to do the same. Feel free to integrate prayers for your companion into your own prayer life, however it works best.

Worship: Invite your companion to sit with you for worship. Certainly look for him or her on Sunday mornings, or whenever you are at the church together. Some visitors who are new to the Christian faith may have questions about worship, or need help finding their way around the bulletin or hymn/song book or Bible.

***Lectio Divina*:** This ancient method of Bible study engages the Scriptures in a prayerful and personal way, inviting reflection and active listening for

God's Word in our lives. If you and your companion have an opportunity to participate in a *Lectio Divina* group, at our church or elsewhere, you are strongly encouraged to do so. If you have interest in being trained to lead a *Lectio Divina* group, let your pastor or *Companions* coordinator know.

Meet: Decide with your companion on a time and a place to meet each week. This can be any place and time you choose. If you need to miss a week because of travel or work or illness or whatever, just pick it up the next week. Don't try to "double up" and do two conversations in one meeting. There are eight conversations; you can complete them in eight weeks, or take a few extra weeks if that works better for your schedules.

Starting where we are: People come to the church out of many different needs and backgrounds. Pairing them with a member companion allows for flexibility to meet different people wherever they are in their walk with God. Your ministry is to invite open talk about the faith, encourage asking questions, and practice honest sharing. Meet people where they are, and help them discern where God is leading. Ask for whatever help you need from your pastors and church leaders.

Conversation: "Conversation is the way humans think together," says business consultant Margaret Wheatley. Your weekly conversations will focus on different aspects of a life of discipleship. A simple prompting or guide for each conversation is included in your packet. This is a two-way street: listen to your companion's unfolding story, *and* invite your companion to get to know you and your story.

Word-Share-Prayer: For each week, there is a Scripture reading, several questions to invite sharing, and an invitation to pray together. This format will work best if you take five to ten minutes of quiet first, for each of you to read through the passage and the questions on your own, and jot down responses that come to mind. Then share. You may also want to have a Bible handy.

Topics: There are eight weeks of conversations. Two of them will happen at the two group gatherings (see "Gatherings" below). The other six follow an ordered sequence:

1. Vocation: The Rhythms of Living

2. Prayer: A Way of Knowing God

3. Forgiveness: A Way of Loving Neighbors

4. Gratitude: A Way of Living with Things

5. Community: Belonging to One Another

6. Calling: Sent to Serve the World

Sharing: The sharing questions for each week go in several different directions, some of which may be more compelling for the two of you than others. Let the conversation go where it needs to go, rather than being overly concerned to cover everything. Look for opportunities to go deeper as your friendship grows. The headings for each week can help you not get sidetracked too far afield.

Prayers: Don't skip the "praying for each other" part! While this will come easier for some than others, you as the member companion should take the initiative each week to conclude your conversation with prayer. Some weeks there is a suggested prayer you can use, if that's helpful, along with the encouragement to pray informally. Using your daily prayer card is also an option. Pray for your companion, and encourage your companion to pray for you.

Gatherings: Two group gatherings with the pastor(s) and other pairs of companions will focus on the Bible and Christian beliefs. Each gathering will include a presentation/discussion, and a paired conversation with your companion in the same Word–Share–Prayer format as the other six weeks.

A. Scripture: The Story and Our Stories

B. Belief: Who Is This Jesus?

Baptism: Anyone considering church membership, whether it's for the first time or at a transition between churches, is taking a new step on their faith journey. Some will come seeking to be baptized. Others may be looking to re-engage the meaning of their baptism. In addition, each of you is taking a step to deepen your baptism by serving as a member companion. The thread tying all of us together is baptism, and our common desire to live into that baptism, day by day by day.

Church council: After you have completed the series of conversations, let the pastor know if your companion would like to meet with congregational leaders to join the church. You may be asked to attend that meeting with your companion and to introduce him or her to those gathered.

Worship: You will be asked to stand with your companion in worship at two different points: at the beginning, when he or she is introduced to the congregation; and at the end if he or she is united with the church as a member. At the introduction, you will be asked to promise that you will be a faithful companion. At the reception into membership, you may be asked to introduce your companion briefly to the congregation, to offer a prayer for him or her, or to lay hands on him or her in prayer and encouragement.

Purpose: While *Companions* has been designed specifically to help church newcomers explore Christian faith, discipleship, and church membership, its broader purpose is to strengthen discipleship across the church. You are encouraged to enter into *Companions* prayerfully, and with the expectation that *you* are going to grow in *your own* faith. In this new relationship, God has good gifts to offer to you, as well as to your newcomer companion.

THE CONVERSATIONS

1. Vocation
The Rhythms of Living

WORD: Read Mark 1:32–38

> That evening, at sundown, they brought to Jesus all who were sick or possessed with demons. And the whole city was gathered around the door. And he cured many who were sick with various diseases, and cast out many demons; and he would not permit the demons to speak, because they knew him. In the morning, while it was still very dark, he got up and went out to a deserted place, and there he prayed. And Simon and his companions hunted for him. When they found him, they said to him, "Everyone is searching for you." He answered, "Let us go on to the neighboring towns, so that I may proclaim the message there also, for that is what I came out to do." (NRSV)

SHARE

In the midst of a demanding ministry, Jesus sought time alone with God. Why was that important for him?

Tell each other about who you are and what you do all week—both out in the world and at home with your family. In what sense is this vocation a ministry for you?

What do you like to do for fun? Is God there somewhere in your play?

Describe your idea of a renewing, restful "sabbath"—where do you find that in your life?

When are you alone? When do you experience silence? Are these positive experiences for you? In what way?

Share how you balance work and play, job and family, activity and rest, in your life. In what ways is that balance hard for you to maintain? What benefits does it give you?

PRAYER

Share any particular needs for prayer.
You may want to begin with this prayer from Psalms 42 and 63:

> *As the deer longs for the water-brooks, so my soul longs for you, O God.*
>
> *O God, you are my God; eagerly I seek you;*
> *My soul thirsts for you, my flesh faints for you,*
> *as in a barren and dry land where there is no water . . .*
> *For your loving kindness is better than life itself; my lips shall give you praise.*
> *So will I bless you as long as I live and lift up my hands in your name.*

Pray for each other, especially around the things you have shared together today.

2. Prayer
A Way of Knowing God

WORD: Read Philippians 4:4-9

> Rejoice in the Lord always. I will say it again: Rejoice! Let your gentleness be evident to all. The Lord is near. Do not be anxious about anything, but in every situation, by prayer and petition, with thanksgiving, present your requests to God. And the peace of God, which transcends all understanding, will guard your hearts and your minds in Christ Jesus. Finally, brothers and sisters, whatever is true, whatever is noble, whatever is right, whatever is pure, whatever is lovely, whatever is admirable—if anything is excellent or praiseworthy—think about such things. Whatever you have learned or received or heard from me, or seen in me—put it into practice, and the God of peace will be with you. (TNIV)

SHARE

In some situations, it's hard to pray "with thanksgiving." Can you think of a time when gratitude helped? How about a time when anxiety won?

Share the patterns you have tried for establishing a life of prayer—times of day, special places, particular prayers or practices. What's worked for you? What hasn't worked?

Where are you satisfied with your prayer life? Where are you frustrated, or needing to grow?

Does reading Scripture help you pray and be with God? Does it help you "encounter" Jesus or "hear" God's voice? How?

Memorizing a psalm means you can pray it anytime. Share any psalms you know by heart. If you like, learn Psalm 100 or 63:1-8 for morning, and Psalm 139:1-12 for bedtime.

Reflect on your experience so far of praying for each other daily. What's that been like?

PRAYER

Share any special needs for prayer this week.
Pray for one another, especially around the things you have shared today.
Conclude with the prayer Jesus taught (Matthew 6:5-13; Luke 11:1-4). You might try this ecumenical version:

> *Our Father in heaven,*
> *hallowed be your name,*
> *your kingdom come,*
> *your will be done on earth as in heaven.*
> *Give us today our daily bread.*
> *Forgive us our sins as we forgive those who sin against us.*
> *Save us from the time of trial, and deliver us from evil.*
> *For the kingdom, the power and the glory are yours, now and forever. Amen.*

3. Forgiveness
A Way of Loving Neighbors

WORD: Read Matthew 18:15-22

> "If a fellow believer hurts you, go and tell him—work it out between the two of you. If he listens, you've made a friend. If he won't listen, take one or two others along so that the presence of witnesses will keep things honest, and try again. If he still won't listen, tell the church. If he won't listen to the church, you'll have to start over from scratch, confront him with the need for repentance, and offer again God's forgiving love. Take this most seriously: A yes on earth is yes in heaven; a no on earth is no in heaven. What you say to one another is eternal. I mean this. When two of you get together on anything at all on earth and make a prayer of it, my Father in heaven goes into action. And when two or three of you are together because of me, you can be sure that I'll be there."
>
> At that point, Peter got up the nerve to ask, "Master, how many times do I forgive a brother or sister who hurts me? Seven?"
>
> Jesus replied, "Seven! Hardly. Try seventy times seven." (*The Message*)

SHARE

Why do you suppose the Gospels make such a big deal about forgiveness? Are the relationships we have with other people that important? Why?

Share a time when you hurt someone else, and instead of the retaliation you feared, you were forgiven. Did that experience change you in some way?

Share a time when you were unable to forgive someone else, or when someone refused to forgive you. What did that make you feel, think, do? How has that experience shaped you?

Is there an ongoing relationship in your life that is unreconciled? What could you do to make peace? What do you need to leave in God's hands for now? You might want to pray for this person as you conclude today.

Think about the relationships you have that are going *right*. What makes them strong?

Where have you experienced God's forgiveness in your life? How did you know it was real? Are you different now because of that experience? How?

PRAYER

Pray for each other.
Pray for the people you each hold dear.
Pray for the relationships in which there is distance or struggle.
You may want to conclude today's prayers by using your *Companions* daily prayer card.

4. Gratitude
A Way of Living with Things

WORD: Read 2 Corinthians 9:6–8

> Remember this: Whoever sows sparingly will also reap sparingly, and whoever sows generously will also reap generously. Each of you should give what you have decided in your heart to give, not reluctantly or under compulsion, for God loves a cheerful giver. And God is able to bless you abundantly so that in all things at all times, having all that you need, you will abound in every good work. (TNIV)

SHARE

Do you think of yourself as a grateful person? How does that show?
What ways have you found to make a habit of ***gratitude***? How about generosity?
How are gratitude and generosity related—in the verses above? in your own life?

How we relate to our "stuff" can be tricky sometimes. We may want more than we really need. Or it can start to feel like our ***possessions*** own us, rather than the other way around. How does your faith impact the choices you make about material things?

What does ***money*** have to do with being a disciple of Jesus? Talk about how you make decisions regarding your money. How do you decide how much to spend on a vacation? Or budget for food and housing? Or give to the church? Or help out your children?

Writing to the Corinthians, Paul is clear that Christian ***giving*** should be joyful. Have you ever had an experience of giving that gave you great joy? Describe it.
What are some of the things that make giving joyless for you?

What is ***stewardship*** to you? Does stewardship have to do with more than money?
Do you think of yourself as a steward of gifts from God?
How does this impact the way you live?

PRAYER

See if your companion has particular joys to share this week.
Give thanks for one another, and pray about the things you have shared today.
Name the things in your life that you are grateful for.
Speak your gratitude to God, and give thanks for God's good gifts.

5. Community
Belonging to One Another

WORD: Read 1 Corinthians 12:12–14, 24–26

> Just as a body, though one, has many parts, but all its many parts form one body, so it is with Christ. For we were all baptized by one Spirit so as to form one body—whether Jews or Gentiles, slave or free—and we were all given the one Spirit to drink. Even so the body is not made up of one part but of many . . . God has put the body together, giving greater honor to the parts that lacked it, so that there should be no division in the body, but that its parts should have equal concern for each other. If one part suffers, every part suffers with it; if one part is honored, every part rejoices with it. Now you are the body of Christ, and each one of you is a part of it. (TNIV)

SHARE

What difference does it make if you're in church on Sunday? To you? To God? To the church? What does it mean to call the church a covenant community? Based on the passage above, what might Paul say?

Just as it "takes a village to raise a child," it also takes a community to make a Christian. Share how the church and church people have helped shape your faith.

What's the most satisfying thing you've ever been involved in at a church? What made it satisfying?

Consider where you find your "place" in our congregation's life and ministry. Which opportunities for service interest you? What helps you grow as a disciple? What in our worship touches you? What else do you wonder about? (You may want to look through the church website together, or review printed material about the congregation's ministries.)

Share something you appreciate, or a question you have, about the denomination our congregation is a part of.

Members are asked to support the church with their prayers, their presence, their gifts, their study, and their service. Which of these do you do best? Which is easiest to neglect?

PRAYER

See what needs your companion has for prayers this week.
Pray for one another, especially around the things you have shared today.
Pray for the people and ministries of our church.

6. Calling
Sent to Serve the World

WORD: Read Mark 3:13–19

> Jesus went up the mountain and called to him those whom he wanted, and they came to him. And he appointed twelve, whom he also named apostles, to be with him, and to be sent out to proclaim the message, and to have authority to cast out demons. So he appointed the twelve: Simon (to whom he gave the name Peter); James son of Zebedee and John the brother of James (to whom he gave the name Boanerges, that is, Sons of Thunder); and Andrew, and Philip, and Bartholomew, and Matthew, and Thomas, and James son of Alpheus, and Thaddeus, and Simon the Cananaean, and Judas Iscariot, who betrayed him. (NRSV)

SHARE

When Jesus called the Twelve, Mark says he called them to be *with him*, and to be *sent out*. In what ways are you called to be with Jesus? To be sent out?

The word *apostle* means "sent." Tell a story about something/someplace/someone God has sent you to. Did you go? Did you consider not going? What happened?

Like the first apostles, we're sent both to *speak* a good word and to *do* good deeds. How do you serve Christ with your speaking? With your doing?

Well-known author Frederick Buechner once defined vocation as "the place where your deep gladness and the world's deep hunger meet." Where is that for you?

Share how God called you, or is calling you (or maybe isn't calling you), to join with this community of believers? How do/did you know?

What sort of ministry do you sense God is sending you to at the present time? In the church? In the community? In your workplace? In your home?

PRAYER

Share any special needs for prayer this week.
Pray for each other.
You may want to conclude with your *Companions* prayer based on Ephesians 3:16–19:

> *O God, according to the riches of your glory, strengthen _____ and me in our inner being with power through your Holy Spirit. Grant that Christ may dwell in our hearts as we are being rooted and grounded in love. Give us the grace to comprehend, with all the saints, what is the breadth and length and height and depth of the love of Christ, and to know that love, though it surpasses knowledge, until we are filled with all the fullness of your Spirit. Amen.*

A. The Story and Our Stories

For use at Group Gathering A on
"The Bible as One Story"

WORD: Read Deuteronomy 6:4–9

> Hear, O Israel: The Lord is our God, the Lord alone. You shall love the Lord your God with all your heart, and with all your soul, and with all your might. Keep these words that I am commanding you today in your heart. Recite them to your children and talk about them when you are at home and when you are away, when you lie down and when you rise. Bind them as a sign on your hand, fix them as an emblem on your forehead, and write them on the doorposts of your house and on your gates. (NRSV)

SHARE

How much of the Bible have you read?

What parts of the Bible are you most familiar with? What parts of Scripture would you like to become more familiar with?

Are there parts of the Bible you turn to often? For comfort? For guidance? For other things? Which parts have you returned to most frequently?

What does Deuteronomy suggest about how we should make use of God's Word in the rhythms of our daily lives? Do you do any of these? Which ones?

Have you ever put a Bible verse on the refrigerator or in a frame on your wall or carried a cross in your pocket? How do these or other tangible reminders of God's Word help you?

Share a biblical character you are especially drawn to, or see something of yourself in. Share a favorite Bible passage, and why it is important to you.

PRAYER

Share any joys or concerns for today.
You may want to begin with this portion of Psalm 19:

> *The law of the LORD is perfect and revives the soul;*
> *The testimony of the LORD is sure and gives wisdom to the innocent.*
> *The statutes of the LORD are just and rejoice the heart;*
> *The commandment of the Lord is clear and gives light to the eyes . . .*
> *By them also is your servant enlightened,*
> *and in keeping them there is great reward . . .*
> *Let the words of my mouth and the meditation of my heart*
> *be acceptable in your sight,*
> *O LORD, my strength and my redeemer.*

Pray for each other.

A. The Story and Our Stories
For use at Group Gathering A on
"The Bible as One Story" (alternate option)

WORD: "The Bible as One Story"

> *Earlier in the gathering, the biblical story from Genesis to Revelation was told as a single story of salvation, using some form of presentation, reading, drama, video, slide show, time line, hymn sing . . . or a group exercise helped you recall together the key elements and themes of that story. Let this presentation serve as the "Word" for your reflection today.*

SHARE

How much of the Bible have you read?

What parts of the Bible are you most familiar with? What parts of Scripture would you like to become more familiar with?

Share a biblical character you are especially drawn to, or see something of yourself in. Share a favorite Bible passage and why it is important to you.

Psalm 119:105 says, "*Your Word is a lantern to my feet and a light upon my path.*" In what ways have you found this to be true for you? Are there ways it is untrue for you?

If *you* were to describe the whole Bible as one big long story, what would the title be? How about some of the chapter headings?

Share your responses to the presentation on "The Bible as One Story."

PRAYER

Share any joys or concerns for the week.
You may want to begin with this portion of Psalm 19:

> *The law of the LORD is perfect and revives the soul;*
> *The testimony of the LORD is sure and gives wisdom to the innocent.*
> *The statutes of the LORD are just and rejoice the heart;*
> *The commandment of the LORD is clear and gives light to the eyes . . .*
> *By them also is your servant enlightened,*
> *and in keeping them there is great reward . . .*
> *Let the words of my mouth and the meditation of my heart*
> *be acceptable in your sight,*
> *O LORD, my strength and my redeemer.*

Pray for each other.

B. Who Is this Jesus?

For use at Group Gathering B on "What We Believe"

WORD: Read Luke 9:18–23

> Once when Jesus was praying alone, with only the disciples near him, he asked them, "Who do the crowds say that I am?" They answered, "John the Baptist; but others, Elijah; and still others, that one of the ancient prophets has arisen." He said to them, "But who do you say that I am?" Peter answered, "The Messiah of God."
>
> He sternly ordered and commanded them not to tell anyone, saying, "The Son of Man must undergo great suffering, and be rejected by the elders, chief priests, and scribes, and be killed, and on the third day be raised." Then he said to them all, "If any want to become my followers, let them deny themselves and take up their cross daily and follow me." (NRSV)

SHARE

Who do *you* say that Jesus is? Who is Jesus Christ for you?

The church's basic confession is: Jesus Christ is our Lord and Savior.
Talk about how you claim this affirmation for yourself. Where do you struggle with it? How do you try to live it?

How do you understand Jesus' birth, or incarnation? What does his birth tell you about God? What do you admire most about the way Jesus lived his life on earth?

How do you understand Jesus' death and resurrection? What difference did it make—for the world? for you? Share what you're sure about, as well as what you're not so sure of.

How do you know Jesus? Is there an experience you have had that you might describe as an "encounter" with the risen Christ? Where in your life do you "see" Jesus?

PRAYER

Share any special needs for prayer this week.
Pray for each other, especially for growing in faith and friendship with Jesus Christ.
You might want to conclude with this prayer based on Ephesians 1:17–19:

> *God of our Lord Jesus Christ, give to _____ and to me a spirit of wisdom and revelation as we come to know him, so that, with the eyes of our heart enlightened, we each may know what is the hope to which he has called us, what are the riches of his glorious inheritance among the saints, and what is the immeasurable greatness of his power for us who believe. Amen.*

Daily Prayer Card

O God, according to the riches of your glory,
strengthen _____ and me in our inner being
with power through your Holy Spirit.
Grant that Christ may dwell in our hearts
as we are being rooted and grounded in love.
Give us the grace to comprehend, with all the saints,
what is the breadth and length and height and depth of the love of Christ,
and to know that love, though it surpasses knowledge,
until we are filled with all the fullness of your Spirit. Amen.

—based on Ephesians 3:16–19

— — — — — — — — — — — —

Daily Prayer Card

O God, according to the riches of your glory,
strengthen _____ and me in our inner being
with power through your Holy Spirit.
Grant that Christ may dwell in our hearts
as we are being rooted and grounded in love.
Give us the grace to comprehend, with all the saints,
what is the breadth and length and height and depth of the love of Christ,
and to know that love, though it surpasses knowledge,
until we are filled with all the fullness of your Spirit. Amen.

—based on Ephesians 3:16–19

Contact Information Form

Name _____

Address _____

_____

Phone #s _____

Email _____

Fill out this form, and give it to your companion.
Your companion also has a form to provide contact information for you.

6

The Back Story

COMPAÑEROS IN TUCSON, ARIZONA

In May 2007, my husband David and I arrived in Tucson, Arizona, to begin a co-pastorate at Trinity Presbyterian Church. We were excited about an urban ministry in a congregation that, despite a membership roll much diminished from its highpoint in the 1970s, still had a solid core of 250 committed members, good energy and enthusiasm for ministry, and abundant hope of reinventing themselves for a vibrant future. During the four years prior to our arrival, over the course of an extended interim pastorate, much had been put on hold, and the congregation was eager to expand both its mission and its membership.

When we arrived, the only procedure in place for responding to visitor requests for church membership was to convene the church's leadership council and add them to the rolls. There were no "new member classes" or orientation sessions in place, no time given for discernment of God's role in leading a person to a new church (or a church to a new member), and little systematic membership outreach. As it turned out, that provided us with a great opportunity to reframe the church's ministry with visitors, from start to finish. Already convinced of the serious limitations of the "new member class" model, we were happy not to have inherited one! Instead, we set out to design a series of conversations that could be the basis for a more relational, more spiritually grounded, and more communally visible

Companions

companioning ministry with all those who walked through our doors and into our common life. The result was *Companions*—or what we called, in that southwestern congregation, *Compañeros*.

We settled on eight weeks as a long enough time frame to develop a genuine friendship, but not so long as to be burdensome or discourage potential participants. We began with one newly married couple, two graduate students, and two older single women—all of whom had been attending the church since before our arrival. During the first year, three more couples, a young mom, and five other single newcomers took part. We initially trained about a dozen member companions, all of whom worked with at least one assigned newcomer sometime during that first year.

The initial participants, both newcomers and member companions, responded enthusiastically, and *Compañeros* became an ongoing part of the congregation's outreach ministry. Heather and Travis, newly married, found in the Hendersons a couple who opened their home in hospitality, becoming both friends and mentors. A young mom with a two-year-old daughter, discovered in Rosemary, her octogenarian companion, an inspiration to joyful, grateful, generous living. When Rosemary died a year later, her loss was grieved by this new young friend, along with the church's longstanding members. Peggy and Nancy became long-term friends as a result of *Compañeros*. Lori's baptism, at the conclusion of her companioning journey, is one the congregation experienced with great astonishment and celebration.

Over the next six years, *Compañeros* was offered continuously. The number of companion pairs active at any given time slowed down to somewhere between one and three. Some of the member companions who found special joy and calling in this ministry signed on for repeated assignments with the church's newest visitors. Others, content with making one new friend, were replaced by new recruits. Training opportunities were repeated, or on occasion accomplished informally for each newly recruited member companion. And we discovered that some of the church's newest members, who had experienced the companioning conversations as newcomers, made terrific member companions for subsequent visitors! We also found that its flexibility made *Compañeros* helpful to newcomers with particular challenges. A recent immigrant from Togo was greatly eased by having a member companion who was fluent in French. And several single men who had once been homeless were included, encouraged, and supported in ways that were life-changing for them. While occasionally there was resistance (people transferring from other Presbyterian churches, for example, who felt that an eight-week commitment was excessive), most were eager, and in the end grateful, for the gifts of friendship and spiritual growth that a companioning ministry offered them. Over time, both the Trinity congregation and its leadership embraced *Compañeros* as an integral part of "the way we do things at our church."

CLOSING THE "BACK DOOR"

During the seven years I served Trinity as its pastor, we reached over fifty newcomers with the *Compañeros* ministry, and a total of twenty-two church members served as their companions. Of the fifty-one visitors who completed the companioning conversations in those years, forty-six joined the church as members. A few of the those who did not join remained active as visitors, while the rest moved on. But the most remarkable statistic was that, excluding twelve new members who either died or moved away from Tucson, *only one* of the forty-six who joined drifted away from the church and disappeared out "the back door"! At the time I left Trinity in 2014, thirty-three of the new members we had received since 2007 were still active in the church, engaged in its ministries, and in many cases involved in its leadership.

The discovery that *Compañeros* helped to foster long-term, committed church membership did not come as a surprise exactly, but it was a welcome affirmation of what we had been hoping for in an outreach ministry designed around companioning. I believe that the success we had in closing "the back door" was due in large part to the program's primary focus on building meaningful relationships within the context of a spiritual community. Newcomers were enabled to become thoroughly acquainted with the church and its ministry before deciding to join. They became known to the whole congregation over several months through regular invitations to keep them in prayer. They had an opportunity to make one meaningful friend in the church—an initial friendship that most often opened the door to others. And that friendship was deeply rooted—in prayer, Scripture, and honest sharing about the faith and living the Christian life. All these things together contributed to a community in which newcomers were able to find welcome, get connected to others, grow spiritually, become engaged in ministry, and find their place among us. A community in which they felt known, respected, encouraged and supported made them want to stay, and stay committed.

A FESTIVAL OF FAITH

The larger spiritual life of the congregation was also positively impacted by *Compañeros,* although that is harder to measure. One concrete program we tried, once *Compañeros* was well-established, was a congregation-wide event. We could see that the conversations were having a positive impact on the newcomers and their member companions, and we wanted to expand the number of people being exposed to them. So the Growth and Outreach Team planned a one-time "Festival of Faith" event (about one hundred people attended), in which we used the conversation guides to invite one-on-one dialogue and sharing.

It was a Sunday after worship. The sermon that morning had included five to ten minutes for worshipers to do their own reflecting on the lectionary Gospel passage using a Word–Share–Prayer guide prepared for the service, so people were familiar with the format we were going to use. Following worship, the Growth and Outreach Team provided a simple lunch served family-style at tables, after which everyone present was invited to find a conversation partner. They were free to choose a friend they knew well, or someone they hardly knew at all—anyone except their own spouse. Partners paired up, took two chairs to a spot in the fellowship hall where they could sit together, and chose a conversation topic. The list of topics was printed out (it had been artfully incorporated into the placemats for the luncheon) and included eight choices. Four were the Word–Share–Prayer conversation topics from *Compañeros,* slightly reworked for this more general occasion (Vocation, Prayer, Gratitude, and Community), and four others had been prepared specially for the event (Worship, Discipleship, Service, and Justice—see the appendix). No attempt was made to divide the conversation topics up evenly among the participants; we simply allowed for self-selection based on interest. As it turned out, all eight topics were undertaken by at least two sets of partners. Once everyone had the Word–Share–Prayer sheet on their chosen topic and their instructions, thirty minutes were allowed for one-on-one conversations using the conversation guides. A warning was given after twenty-five minutes, to prompt the partners to wrap up their sharing and pray for each other. After the first conversations were completed, we did an "apple cart upset," exchanging partners and conversation topics for a second round. Finally a fifteen-minute wrap-up invited the whole group to reflect on the experience, briefly sharing learnings, surprises, and suggestions.

The congregation responded enthusiastically to this event. Many found the Word–Share–Prayer format conducive to a good conversation because it was, at one and the same time, spiritually direct, experientially concrete, and open-ended. A number of people suggested other conversation topics they would be interested in if additional conversation guides could be prepared. One or two people signed up to be trained as member companions in the future. The Growth and Outreach Team intended to repeat the event, although that did not occur before I left.

STRENGTHENING THE FAITH OF THE CHURCH

The Festival of Faith was one concrete way we sought to make wider congregational use of the companioning ministry resources, and it had a positive impact on the church. But the largest impact, I believe, was from the *Compañeros* outreach ministry itself. By the time I concluded my pastorate at Trinity, about one third of the church's members had engaged in the set of eight companioning conversations, either as newcomers or as member companions (or in some cases both). And that new reality had begun to quietly transform the culture of the whole church. The core spiritual values of *Compañeros* were taking increasingly deeper root. While the value of relationships and community were already strong at Trinity, the congregation grew in their capacities for hospitality, prayer, and discernment. First-time visitors were greeted, not just by a few members assigned to the task, but by many. Prayers in just about every setting became more participatory. And the church's leaders became accustomed to bringing discernment practices to bear on their decision making. It was as if some "tipping point" was in sight, and the experience of a sizable minority began gradually to transform the character of the community. In small, subtle, almost imperceptible ways, the overall spiritual life of the congregation got a little stronger, and baptismal identity and vocation were underscored and strengthened.

Within a safe environment for spiritual conversation, the congregation grew in their comfort level with honest, thoughtful, appropriate talk about God and God's presence in their lives. Finding the words to describe our experience of the sacred is a lifelong project—it can't be hurried, or pigeonholed into theological categories, there are no shortcuts we can take without risking dishonesty. *Compañeros* helped people at Trinity find the words to describe at least parts of their own relationships with God. This in turn led them to test their voices, and helped them grow in the capacity and courage for sharing their experience with others who were eager to hear it. In the end, unless the church's work of evangelism is to be reduced to theological clichés, this is the way the good news of the gospel will be told, and this capacity for comfortable and honest "God-speech"[9] in the church's people is no small thing to nurture.

The final benefit I would note was for the governing council of church leaders. Once *Compañeros* was in place in the life of the congregation, it gave Trinity's leaders a tangible place to direct those who inquired about church membership, and an ordered process they could trust to unfold over a period of time, rather than rushing to receive as a member any visitor who expressed even a casual interest in joining. Because *Compañeros* provided newcomers with the time and personal interaction they needed to explore a serious commitment to Christ and his church, it helped them get clearer about their own interests in church membership, their own gifts for service, and their own readiness to seek baptism or baptismal renewal. At the same time, having such a process in place gave the church leaders confidence that, by directing newcomers to *Compañeros*, they were in fact providing a real and good service to the congregation's visitors, and at the same time they were enabling the church to exercise a faithful outreach ministry of hospitality and spiritual nurture. All of this empowered the church's leadership council, and gave them the sense that they had an outreach ministry that didn't just depend on the pastor or a small committee—it belonged to them and to the congregation as a whole.

An earlier chapter offered half a dozen suggestions for using the *Companions* materials more broadly in the life of the whole congregation (see the "Flexibility and Adaptation" section in chapter 4). At Trinity, we tried some of those ideas, but not all of them. And they did help to expose a larger number in the church to what the conversations were all about. In addition to the Festival of Faith, we used the eight conversations one year as the core of the annual retreat for church leaders. They enjoyed it immensely because it was relational and relaxed. It helped them get to know each other as a new year was beginning, and build the foundation for a solid leadership team. And by giving them practice in articulating something of their

---

9. "God-speech" is Ben Campbell Johnson's term for "candid, spontaneous, natural conversation about the presence and activity of the Creator" (*Speaking of God*, 11).

life with God, it helped them each become a little stronger spiritually. Both the Festival of Faith and the leadership retreat were programmatic ways of using the materials. But less formal applications would also be possible and beneficial. I believe a church that could successfully promote the conversations as a spiritual discipline for any two individuals to undertake together would find its members' faith and Christian practice growing in all kinds of surprising ways.

While *Companions* is designed as an outreach ministry to newcomers, only the imagination limits the ways it might also be used to build up the church and strengthen its faith—transforming lives, growing passionate practicing disciples, and contributing to more spiritually alive congregations.

Appendix
Resources for Leaders

Member Companion Training Session
1½–2 hours

INVITATIONS to member companion training should be extended to those with potential gifts for this ministry. They may be invited to attend, learn what it's all about, and then confirm their willingness to serve.

Introductions (10 minutes)
- Make sure everyone knows each other by name.
- If the group is larger than about eight, name tags may be useful.

Opening Prayer
- If the meeting is around a meal, this can be the table grace.
- Let the conversation be unstructured during the mealtime (allow an additional 30 minutes).

Conversation Exercise in Pairs (30–45 minutes)
- Hand out copies of the first Word–Share–Prayer sheet on vocation.
- Read the Scripture passage aloud to whole group.

Appendix

- Give them 5 minutes individually to jot down responses to the text and to the sharing questions.
- Then pair them up for 20 minutes of conversation with a partner. It is preferable not to pair spouses with each other.
- After 20 minutes, invite them to pray with and for each other using the instructions on the sheet.
- Back in the large group, invite brief reflections on the conversation exercise:
  - What came easy? What felt hard?
  - What surprised them? What did they wonder about?
  - Was there a new insight they gained?

Companions Packets (30–45 minutes)

- You'll see we've just done the first conversation in a set of 8 that make up *Companions*. Hand out packets and orient them briefly to what's inside.
  - A Welcome to *Companions*
  - Member Companion Guidelines
  - 6 numbered Word–Share–Prayer conversation guides
  - 2 lettered Word–Share–Prayer conversation guides, for use at group gatherings
  - 2 prayer cards
  - 1 form for exchange of contact information between companions
- Except for the Member Companion Guidelines, newcomers will receive an identical packet.
  Note: your companion's packet will be given to YOU, so that you may go over it with him or her at your first meeting together. Please do not just pass it along. Rather, take a few minutes to give your companion a brief introduction to what's in it, and how you will use it together.
- Work through the Member Companion Guidelines as a group—making comments, responding to questions, imagining scenarios. Remind participants that their newcomer companions will *not* have this handout. Some things to lift up might include:

Member Companion Training Session

- Note that companions are asked to share personal faith and discipleship, not impart information. No need to be an "expert." If there's a question you can't answer, go find out together. Make use of your pastors and other church leaders; it will help your companion get to know some of them.

- Underscore the importance of prayer, praying daily for each other, praying together each time you meet. Brainstorm with the group how to use the prayer cards.

- If *Lectio Divina* will be offered, note the time and place, and encourage participation by all companions. This ancient Bible study method involves listening to Scripture to hear a living and personal Word from God:
    - it is more devotional than study-oriented.
    - it is prayerful engagement with others rather than group discussion.

- Emphasize listening, starting where people are in their faith. Share your own related experiences. Speak honestly about your struggles and doubts. Model asking good questions over providing right answers.

- Review the sequence of conversations:
    - Note the common Word–Share–Prayer framework.
    - Note the sequence of topics from easy to deeper.
    - Note the gradual movement towards discernment of God's call.

- Invite comment on business consultant Margaret Wheatley's statement: "Conversation is the natural way humans think together."

- With the Word–Share–Prayer sheets, be sure to allow 5–10 minutes of quiet at the beginning for personal reflection—time for each companion to reread the Scripture passage, ponder the reflection questions, jot down initial responses. This way each of you comes to the conversation with a spiritual "readiness" that will foster a richer sharing.

- Don't feel obliged to "cover everything" in the Share section. Rather focus in on those questions and reflection suggestions that seem most compelling for your companion and yourself.

APPENDIX

- The two group gatherings allow for both expanding the newcomer's initial circle of friends, and for establishing a relationship with the church's pastor. They will be scheduled as close to week 3 and week 6 as people's schedules allow, but they may fall at different points in the sequence of 8 conversations for different companion pairs.
- The group gatherings include some teaching about Scripture and Christian belief, as well as a related Word–Share–Prayer conversation for you and your companion. These two conversation sheets will be handed out at the group gatherings. When necessary, this conversation may take place after the gathering.
- Expect surprises. Look to do some growing yourself. And each time you have one of these conversations with a different companion—remember, it'll be a different conversation!

Conclusion (15 minutes)

- Review the basic *Companions* commitment to:
    - **Pray** for each other daily.
    - **Worship** together with the church on Sundays.
    - **Meet together** weekly for a conversation about Christian life and faith.
- Read through the section on the back side of the Welcome sheet about the varied "hopes" for this ministry.
- Note the contact information exchange sheet—you'll need that to be in touch with each other. Make sure you fill it out, give them yours, and ask for theirs.
- Closing comments or questions from anyone?
- Confirm those who would like to be part of this ministry as a member companion (for those still considering, set a deadline for a reply).
- If newcomers to the church have already expressed an interest in having a member companion, assignments may be made at this time.
- Announce or set upcoming dates for introducing these newcomers in worship, and for the first group gathering.

Closing Prayer

Additional Member Training Options:

Lectio Divina (30 minutes)
> *When the church has a* Lectio Divina *group that companions will be encouraged to participate in, you may wish to include this segment as well. In that case, I'd recommend beginning with* Lectio Divina, *moving to the* Companions *packets, and then go to the Conversation Exercise before the final review and conclusion.*

- Do *Lectio Divina* on a passage of Scripture. You will find instructions for group *Lectio Divina* elsewhere in this appendix.
- You might want to choose a passage that begins one of the Word–Share–Prayer conversation guides. Or choose a passage that was read (or will be read) in Sunday's worship. Or choose something else that you believe will be helpful to those considering a member companioning ministry.

Reflection with Experienced Member Companions (20 minutes)
> *When this training session is repeated to recruit additional member companions, it can be useful to invite several experienced companions to share a bit of their experience:*

- something they appreciated, or felt they gained, from the experience;
- a difficult situation they encountered and how they handled it;
- any advice they would give to others doing this ministry.

Group Gathering A
The Bible as One Story

Meeting Outline (2 hours)

Introductions (10 minutes)
- Make sure everyone has met everyone else (nametags may help).
- If an "icebreaker" would be useful, invite each person to share their name, where they're from, and either a favorite Bible passage or a biblical character they identify with.

Opening Prayer

Checking In (15 minutes)
- Get a sense of where the companion pairs are, what their experience has been:
  - How often have they met? How many conversations completed?
  - Which conversations have been most interesting? any troubling?
  - Who's doing *Lectio Divina*?
  - How about praying daily for each other? How's that going?

The Bible as One Story (40 minutes)
- Offer a presentation on the broad story of salvation that is told in Scripture from Genesis to Revelation. Be creative. Reading, drama, video, slide show, timeline, hymn sing—anything can work to pull the many stories of the Bible together into one overarching story of God's love for a people.
- I often used a Presbyterian resource called *The One Story of the Bible*.[1] It lays out a series of themes—from creation and fall, to promise and bondage, exodus and exile, to fulfillment, love, resurrection and church—to convey the rhythms of human faithfulness and failure, of

---
1. Hainer, "One Story," 65–85.

divine judgment and ultimate mercy, that are the recurring milemarkers of both the biblical story and our own.

- Sometimes I did this not as a presentation but as a group exercise. We created a timeline of biblical events, recalling together the key elements and themes of Scripture's story, and when we were done, took note of the recurring patterns in it.
- Another way to do it is to use some of the passages where Scripture itself calls to mind the big-picture story: from Hebrew worship in Deuteronomy 26:5–10, or Miriam's praise for deliverance in Exodus 15:1–8; from Peter preaching the good news in Acts 2:22–36, or Paul defending himself in Acts 13:16–39, or Stephen just before he was martyred in Acts 7:2–53.
- These are just a few possibilities. There are numerous resources available, perhaps even some your denomination offers. The idea is not to get too concerned about all the details (this is not a cram course in biblical content!), but rather to see the broad strokes of the human story with God, and to affirm how the biblical story intersects with our own.

Companion Conversations (45 minutes)

- Hand out the Word–Share–Prayer sheet for group gathering A, "The Story and Our Stories" (or invite companions to find it in their packets).
- If you haven't already, you'll need to decide which of two alternatives to use:
  - The first begins, like all the others, with reflection on a passage of Scripture.
  - The alternate includes reflection on the presentation they have just heard.
  - The questions in the Sharing section also vary slightly.
  - The first option should be in their packets; if you want to use the alternate, it will need to be handed out at the gathering.
- Invite member and newcomer companions to pair up, find a quiet spot to sit together, and have a conversation. Note: the time frame will be a little shorter than their weekly conversations: 30–35 minutes

Appendix

(figure 5–10 minutes of quiet reflection on passage and questions, 15–25 minutes of sharing, 5–10 minutes for prayers).

- When back in the large group, gather a brief "taste" of the conversations:
  - Something encouraging you learned about your companion?
  - Something surprising you discovered about the Bible?
- Note: If there are unavoidable time constraints, each companion pair may be asked to complete this conversation when they meet together next, and then pick up the numbered sequence of conversations where they left off on the following week.

Conclusion (10 minutes)

- Take care of any *Companions* "housekeeping" items—upcoming dates, etc.
- See if there are questions or comments from any in the group.

Closing Prayer

Note: You could consider using Psalm 19, from today's Word–Share–Prayer sheet as the closing prayer for the gathering.

Group Gathering B
What We Believe

Meeting Outline (2 hours)

Introductions (10 minutes)
- Make sure everyone has met everyone else (name tags may help).
- Invite each person to identify something they've always wanted to know about the faith or the church *(. . .but were afraid to ask?)* Record these questions in some visible place; you can respond to them later in the gathering.

Opening Prayer

Classic Christian Faith—a Review (20 minutes)
- The earliest creed of the church was a simple one: *Jesus is Lord!* (see Romans 10:9).
- Later this was expanded into the fully Trinitarian faith of the Apostles' Creed, early versions of which were in use in baptismal liturgies at the start of the second century. In that context, the creed took a question/answer form (a handout may be prepared for participants displaying the creed and baptismal vows below):

Do you believe in God?
I believe in God, the Father Almighty,
creator of heaven and earth.

Do you believe in Jesus Christ?
I believe in Jesus Christ, God's only Son, our Lord,
who was conceived by the Holy Spirit,
born of the Virgin Mary,
suffered under Pontius Pilate,
was crucified, died, and was buried;
he descended to the dead.

Appendix

On the third day, he rose again;
he ascended into heaven,
he is seated at the right hand of the Father,
and he will come to judge the living and the dead.

Do you believe in the Holy Spirit?
I believe in the Holy Spirit, the holy catholic church,
the communion of saints, the forgiveness of sins,
the resurrection of the body, and the life everlasting.

- Today's profession of faith at baptism includes the reciting of the creed along with a set of vows. The vows, although stated differently in different parts of the church, still invite commitment not to a specific Christian denomination, but to our common Christian faith, to Christ and his church. In the Presbyterian Church, these vows are (substitute the baptismal vows in your own church):

    Trusting in the gracious mercy of God,
    do you turn from the ways of sin
    and renounce evil and its power in the world?

    Do you turn to Jesus Christ
    and accept him as your Lord and Savior
    trusting in his grace and love?

    Will you be Christ's faithful disciple
    obeying his Word and showing his love?

    Will you be a faithful member of this congregation?
    Will you share in its worship and ministry
    through your presence and your prayers,
    your gifts, your study and your service,
    and so fulfill your calling to be a disciple of Jesus Christ?[2]

- Note similarities and differences between the Apostles' Creed and your church's baptismal promises. Allow folks to ask questions and explore meanings of the church's faith. Some of the questions the group raised at the beginning may be appropriate to respond to here.

---

2. Adapted from the *Book of Common Worship*, 407–9.

Companion Conversations (45 minutes)
- Hand out the Word–Share–Prayer sheet for group gathering B, "Who is this Jesus?" (or invite companions to find it in their packets).
- Invite member and newcomer companions to pair up, find a quiet spot to sit together, and have a conversation. Note: the time frame will be a little shorter than their weekly conversations: 30–35 minutes (figure 5–10 minutes of quiet reflection on passage and questions, 15–20 minutes of sharing, 5–10 minutes for prayers).
- When back in the large group, gather a brief "taste" of the conversations:
  - What affirmations about Jesus are clear and comfortable for us?
  - Where are the struggles we have with what we believe and experience?
- Note: If there are unavoidable time constraints, each companion pair may be asked to complete this conversation when they meet together next, and then pick up the numbered sequence of conversations where they left off on the following week.

The Faith of the Whole Church (30 minutes)
This presentation is based on 3 paragraphs in the constitution of the Presbyterian Church: Book of Order, *"The Church and its Confessions" (F-2.03–2.05). But the ideas are applicable and adaptable to other denominational contexts.*
- *All Christians* (Protestant, Catholic, Pentecostal, Orthodox) share a belief in the 2 central mysteries of the faith: the incarnation and the Trinity.
  - *Incarnation*: the Word made flesh in Jesus of Nazareth (celebrated in the Advent/Christmas/Epiphany portion of the church year)
  - *Trinity*: the post-resurrection belief in one God in three persons, Father, Son, and Holy Spirit, and the mystery of Christ's resurrection from death (celebrated in the Lent/Easter/Pentecost portion of the church year)
- *All Protestant Christians* share these 3 convictions from the faith of the sixteenth-century Reformation:

Appendix

- *Grace alone*: We are saved by grace through faith. We cannot earn our salvation by doing good works or supporting the church. Salvation is a gift freely given to us by a loving God; faith (that is, trust) is all that is needed to receive it.
- *Faith alone*: Personal faith gives us access to our God in Christ; communication with God may be accomplished without the mediation of an ordained priest; God hears the prayers of the faithful directly.
- *Scripture alone*: Scripture is the rule for Christian faith and life. By the work of the Holy Spirit in the church, the Bible is a unique witness to the Gospel's good news, and is authoritative for Christian living.

- *Reformed and Presbyterian Christians* tend to emphasize the importance of these 6 beliefs (those in other traditions will want to substitute your own list of central convictions):
  - that God is *sovereign* and Lord of all history;
  - that God's people are *elected* (chosen) not for special privilege, but for salvation and service;
  - that participation in the *covenant* life of the Christian community, the church, is an integral part of Christian faith;
  - that since all we have comes from God, God's people are called to be good *stewards* of all of life;
  - that our tendency to idolatry, placing ourselves above God, deceives us into thinking we are without sin; but *sin* is real and pervasive, destroying human lives and community;
  - that the Christian faith is about *justice* and social transformation, as much as it is about salvation and personal piety.
- Again, allow folks to ask questions and explore meanings of the church's faith. If some of the questions the group raised at the beginning have not yet been addressed, respond to them here.

Checking In/Conclusion (15 minutes)

- Get a sense of where the companion pairs are, what their experience has been:
  - How often have they met? How many conversations completed?

- Which conversations have been most energizing, fruitful, interesting, helpful?
- Have any been disturbing, difficult, boring?
• Take care of any housekeeping items—upcoming dates? Companions nearing completion of their conversations? Anyone ready to join the church?

Closing Prayer

Lectio Divina
A Simple Process for Doing Lectio Divina in a Group

Initial Explanation:

The same passage of Scripture will be read 3 times.

Each time, there will be instructions about what to listen for.

Each reading will be followed by several minutes of silence.

A chime (or other appropriate cue) will conclude the silence and invite any who wish to share their responses briefly.

Simple questions may be asked or affirmations expressed, but discussion is not encouraged.

READ

Invite group members to listen:

Listen, as the passage is read the first time, for the word or phrase that catches your attention, beckons or draws you, surprises you, unnerves or disturbs you.

Read the chosen passage aloud slowly.

Keep silence for 3–5 minutes.

Invite participants to share their single word or phrase.

REFLECT

Invite the group to listen:

Listen, as the passage is read again: Do the words evoke an image? a feeling? What thoughts arise? How does the reading connect with your life now?

Read the passage aloud slowly (or invite a group member to read it).

Keep silence for 3–5 minutes.

Invite brief sharing of the images, feelings, connections that were noticed.

RESPOND

Invite the group to listen:

Listen, as the passage is read the last time, for its invitation to you from God. Is God nudging you to do something? To be something? Is there a message you are hearing? How do you want to respond to God?

Read the passage aloud slowly (or invite a group member to read it).

Keep silence for 5–10 minutes.

Invite sharing. If participants wish to respond to each other, encourage "I hear . . ." or "I wonder . . ." statements that prompt deeper exploration.

REST

Invite the group into a final moment of silence:

Let's sit quietly with God to absorb what we have heard, and to give God thanks. Enjoy God's loving company. Rest in God's presence.

Keep silence for 1–2 minutes, or whatever time seems appropriate.

Pray a simple blessing on all (or invite the group to join in a circle prayer).

The following may be printed and cut as a bookmark:

Lectio Divina

<u>Read</u>
Read slowly. Read
aloud. Listen deeply.
Let the words linger
and sink in.
**What single word
or phrase draws your
attention?**

<u>Reflect</u>
Explore the message.
Do the words evoke an
image? a feeling?
Ruminate, ponder.
What thoughts arise?
**How does this Word
connect with your life?**

<u>Respond</u>
Let your heart
respond to God.
Is God leading you to a
new awareness?
nudging you to take
some action?
offering you a gift?
**What is God inviting
you to do? to be? How do
you want to respond?**

<u>Rest</u>
Savor the silence.
Rest in God's presence.
Surrender to God's
love for you. Enjoy
just being with God.
This is the *"Amen"*
of the prayer.

Baptismal Preparation Session
Exploring the Meanings of Christian Baptism

This outline provides suggestions for an additional meeting with newcomers who have never been baptized. It is intended to be led by the pastor. Member companions are encouraged to attend with their partners. Suggestions offered here will need to be adjusted to fit your particular denominational and congregational patterns for baptismal preparation.

Water

- Invite reflection on experiences with water:
    - Where do you experience water in your daily living?
    - What's one of the most powerful experiences you've ever had with water?
    - In what ways might you connect any of these experiences with baptism?

Scripture

- Try and name together stories from Scripture about water that might inform our understanding of Christian baptism. The following is a partial list, which can be used to prompt memory, if needed:
    - creation out of chaos
    - the great flood
    - crossing the Red Sea—freedom from captivity
    - water from the rock
    - crossing the Jordan—entering the promised land
    - the prophetic call for justice to roll down like waters
    - the baptism of Jesus
    - the woman at the well and Jesus' gift of living water
    - the healing at the pool

- the river flowing through the city of God, healing the nations

Baptism
- Start with Augustine's classic definition of a sacrament as a sign: "an outward and visible sign of an inward and spiritual grace."
  - A sacrament is a sign: one thing that points to something else (like a road sign), a material object that points to a spiritual reality.
- Ask: What then is water a sign of? Create a "cluster chart" brainstorming a variety of the words we might associate with water (shower, bath, drink, thirst, plants, swimming, rain, river, ocean, flood, tsunami . . .)
  - Link related words together into broad categories that describe what water is for us and how we relate to it.
  - Categories might include these: washing, life, death, refreshment . . .
- Consider together how we might understand some of the meanings of Christian baptism, related to the sign of water. Here are some of the basic possibilities that might be included in your conversation:
  - Washing:
    cleansing from sin
    forgiveness
  - Death:
    letting go of an old way of life
    dying with Christ
  - Life:
    new life in Christ
    rising with Christ
    illumination in Christ
    new birth by water and the Spirit
  - Refreshment/Quenching Thirst:
    anointing for **ministry**
    gifts of the **Spirit**
    sealing by the Spirit
    incorporation into the **body of Christ**
    adoption into the covenant community of the church
    freedom from captivity to sin and death

BAPTISMAL PREPARATION SESSION

Faith

- Recall that baptism is intimately connected to faith—
  - both individual faith, and the faith of the church.
  - Either baptism or faith may come first in our experience, but they are linked: people come to personal faith, not in isolation, but through some kind of contact with the faith of the church.
- Review the profession of faith that the church makes in baptism. (The vows that follow are from the Presbyterian service of baptism; you will want to substitute the baptismal vows in your own church.)

> Trusting in the gracious mercy of God,
> do you turn from the ways of sin
> and renounce evil and its power in the world?
>
> Do you turn to Jesus Christ
> and accept him as your Lord and Savior,
> trusting in his grace and love?
>
> Will you be Christ's faithful disciple,
> obeying his Word and showing his love?
>
> *The Apostle's Creed is professed together with the gathered congregation.*
>
> Will you be a faithful member of this congregation?
> Will you share in its worship and ministry
> through your presence and your prayers,
> your gifts, your study and your service,
> and so fulfill your calling to be a disciple of Jesus Christ?[3]

  - Note the language, in the first two questions, of turning away from and turning towards. This is spatial language, a reminder that the promises of baptism are not just about new ways of *understanding* the faith, they are about new ways of *living* it. We agree to "turn" in some new directions in our living, towards some things, away from others.
  - Talk together about the questions and how we answer them.

3. Adapted from the *Book of Common Worship*, 407–9.

Appendix

What Next?

- Reflect together on each newcomer's desire and readiness for baptism:
  - What questions remain to be explored? What else is needed?
  - Make plans for whatever next steps will be helpful.
- Once the *Companions* conversations have been completed, and any other follow-up plans undertaken, the newcomers may request baptism and church membership if they so desire.

SAMPLE LETTERS AND PUBLICITY

Sample Letter to Recent Visitors

This letter is intended to be sent to a visitor who has attended worship for several Sundays in a row.

Dear _____,

We are delighted to see that you have joined us at _____ Church on several Sundays now, and hope you are finding a good welcome among this community and support for your spiritual journey in our worship. We write to invite you to consider participating in our *Companions* program.

Companions is our way of encouraging visitors to reflect on the spiritual journey, and consider the possibility of membership in the body of Christ through our church family. It's an eight-week opportunity to have a conversation companion with whom to visit about faith, discipleship, and church life; someone to pray with and explore the directions God is leading you at this point in your life.

Participating in *Companions* does not assume you have decided to make this your church home; rather, we hope to offer you an opportunity to test that possibility. By inviting you into a friendship with a member companion, into reflection and prayer together, and into broader participation in the life of the church, we hope you will be better able to see whether or not this is the church home for you.

One of us will plan to call you in about a week, to see if you are ready for a member companion. Meanwhile we welcome your presence in worship. We encourage you to get involved in other groups in the church that will meet your needs for Christian growth and fellowship. And we would welcome you as a member of Christ's church at _____, if that is where God's Spirit is leading you.

Blessings to you always.

Faithfully,

To be signed by the church's pastor and/or the Companions *coordinator*

Sample Invitation to Member Companion Training

This letter is intended to be sent to active church members with potential gifts for a companioning ministry with newcomers.

Dear _____,

Our church is getting ready to begin a new membership exploration ministry for visitors called *Companions*. Visitors will be paired with church members for eight weeks of conversation about various aspects of Christian faith and discipleship. This is an outreach ministry that we believe will offer the church's hospitality to the newcomers among us, helping them make an initial friend in the congregation. In addition, *Companions* will help our visitors learn more about our church, reflect on their own faith convictions, questions, and practices with a fellow disciple, and become more aware of what God may be up to in their lives now.

You are receiving this letter for one of two reasons. Either you have expressed an interest in being a member companion, or we believe you have gifts to offer in this ministry and want to encourage you to consider serving in *Companions* in the coming year.

We are inviting you to a (lunch) meeting about *Companions* on:
date, time, and place

The meeting will include an overview of this ministry, along with an opportunity to look at the materials, experiment with the conversations, and ask questions. We'll talk about what to expect as a member companion, and how to handle some typical situations that may arise with newcomers to our fellowship.

Please let the church office know if you'll be attending. If you have questions, you're welcome to give any of us a call. You do not have to make a commitment to being a member companion in order to come to the meeting. Come listen and learn, and then you can let us know if you feel this

Appendix

ministry is for you. If you decide it is, we believe you'll be in for an exciting adventure that will help you grow in your own faith as well!

    Thank you.

Faithfully,

To be signed by the church's pastor and/or the Companions *coordinator and/or representatives of an outreach/evangelism or spiritual nurture committee*

Sample Newsletter or Website Publicity

Visitors to the church are welcome to take part in any of our ministries of worship, discipleship and service. In addition, we invite you to participate in a special ministry designed to help you take some next steps on your spiritual journey.

If you would like to learn more about our ministry . . .

If you'd like to make a friend in this congregation . . .

*If you are looking for guidance as you explore
where God may be leading you next . . .*

*If you are interested in deepening your faith
and your involvement in the church . . .*

*If you've never been part of a church
and want to learn about the Christian faith . . .*

*If you've never been baptized
and believe you would like to receive baptism . . .*

. . . consider enrolling in *Companions*,
our newcomer companioning program.

Those who desire to explore a deeper relationship with God or a new commitment to the church are encouraged to take part in *Companions*. This program pairs an interested visitor with a church member for several weeks of conversation and prayer. It includes the following components:

- a public welcome in worship
- 8 weekly conversations with a member companion
- daily prayer for each other
- weekly worship and study with the church
- 2 gatherings with a pastor and other companions
- baptismal preparation for those not yet baptized as Christians
- an opportunity, if desired, to meet with church leaders to join the church
- baptismal renewal in worship to receive new church members

Appendix

Our hope is that this companion relationship will:

- help you get fully integrated into the life of the church
- build friendships that strengthen the whole body
- take seriously what God is doing in your life now
- encourage honest sharing, asking questions, talking about faith
- start where you are on your spiritual journey and help you take next steps
- help you consider where God is calling you into fellowship and service
- strengthen all participants in faith and discipleship

Companions offers all those who enter our doors a way to grow spiritually, whether or not it leads to church membership.

Sample Sunday Reminders or Announcements

These brief announcements may be used in Sunday bulletins and other church publications. If any are helpful, feel free to adapt to your setting, or just let them be grist for the mill as you fashion your own communication strategy for Companions.

VISITORS: If you're curious to learn more about this community of faith, we encourage you to take part in *Companions*. We'll introduce you to a church member for an eight-week set of conversations about Christian faith and discipleship. Please speak to one of the pastors to learn more.

VISITORS: If you think you might be interested in joining the church, we invite you to sign up for *Companions*. You'll be paired up with a church member for eight weeks of conversation about the faith, the church, and the spiritual life. Please contact our *Companions* coordinator *(give contact information)* to get connected.

VISITORS: Those who desire to explore a deeper relationship with God or a new commitment to the church are encouraged to take part in our companioning program. *Companions* pairs an interested visitor with a church member for several weeks of conversation and prayer. Ask us about it.

OPEN INVITATION: A group of *Companions* are meeting to talk about "The Bible as One Story." Others in the congregation are welcome to join us *(note date, time, and place)*. You'll get to know some of our newcomers, and see this vital ministry of companioning in action.

OPEN INVITATION: A group of *Companions* are meeting to talk about "What We Believe." Others in the congregation are welcome to join us *(note date, time, and place)*. You'll get to know some of our newcomers, and be part of this vital ministry of companioning.

NEW COMPANIONS: Today you will meet *(name)*, who will join member companion *(name)* in exploring God's love and leading. Please keep them both in your prayers over the coming weeks.

APPENDIX

FOR PRAYERS: Please keep these newcomers and their member companions in your prayers as together they explore God's love and leading: *(name)* and his/her member companion *(name)* . . .

RENEWING *HIS/HER* BAPTISM and being received into church membership today is *(name)*, by reaffirmation of his/her faith (or by transfer from another congregation). *His/her* companion for the past eight weeks has been *(name)*. We welcome *(name)* into our community's life and ministry.

RECEIVING THE SACRAMENT OF BAPTISM today is *(name)*. *His/her* companion in faith for the past eight weeks has been *(name)*. We rejoice with *(name)* as *s/he* professes faith and becomes one with Christ and his church.

Church Council Meeting to Receive New Members

In congregations where a governing board or council acts to receive newcomers into church membership, the following process may be suggestive of some helpful possibilities.

Invite the newcomer and his/her member companion to attend the first 30–45 minutes of the meeting. Begin with opening prayers/devotions according to the council's normal pattern, and then proceed to conversation with the new member(s).

- Invite the member companion to briefly introduce the newcomer to the church leaders. This may include ordinary things like the newcomer's name, where they're from, how long they've been attending the church, something about their family, their work, etc.

- Next invite the newcomer to reflect a bit on their own faith and Christian experience. What story might they tell about a previous church experience that was especially formative for them? Are they new to the church and its faith? What has brought them to this church? What has the Spirit of God been up to in their life lately?

- Finally, invite the church leaders to respond with affirmations and/or questions. They might want to follow up on something they heard, or ask about a newcomer's gifts and interests in Christian service. Encourage them to ask questions that will help them as leaders to provide, in the best way possible, for the spiritual nurture of this newcomer as s/he becomes a member of the church.

- At some point, someone should ask about their *Companions* conversations: Was there some learning? A particular insight? Can they recall an especially good conversation? In what ways are they being transformed by God through involvement with this church?

- When the church leaders appear ready, invite the appropriate official action regarding church membership, and then lead the group in prayer for the new member and for the church.

Appendix

- Before dismissing the new member and his/her companion, be sure to set a date for the service of baptismal renewal (or the sacrament of baptism if the newcomer has not been baptized) and public welcome into church membership.

LITURGIES

Introduction of Companions in Faith

This liturgy is for use when newcomers are first paired up with a member companion, as a way to introduce the newcomer to the congregation. It takes place in Sunday worship, ordinarily following the reading and preaching of the Word and before the celebration of the Lord's Supper. Participants are invited to gather near the baptismal font, which shall be open and filled with water.

When several newcomers are being introduced at once, the wording may be adjusted accordingly

Opening
"Jesus said: 'I do not call you servants . . .
but I have called you friends.'"

—*John 15:15*

The newcomer may be briefly introduced.

Today I want to invite you to get to know *(name)*
and to pray for *him/her* over the next weeks,
as *s/he* explores *his/her* own Christian faith and discipleship,
and discerns whether this is a community
where God is calling *him/her* into fellowship and service.

Question to Member Companion
(Name) will be *his/her* companion
in exploring Christian faith and discipleship,
and I ask *him/her* now to make this promise:
> *(Name)*, will you seek to be a faithful companion,
> offering yourself in Christian friendship,
> sharing your own faith openly,
> and encouraging *(name)* in *his/her* walk with God?
> **I will.** Or, **I will, with God's help.**

Introduction of Companions in Faith

Prayer
Let us pray . . .
Faithful God, in baptism you claim us,
and by your Spirit you are working in our lives.
We thank you for leading *(name)* to this time and place.
Guide *him/her* by your Spirit,
that together with *his/her* companion and with your whole church,
s/he may grow in faith, hope and love,
and be a faithful disciple of Jesus Christ,
to whom, with you and the Holy Spirit, be all honor and glory.[4]

*The pastor and the member companion may lay hands
on the newcomer's head or shoulder. If more than one newcomer is being
introduced, the prayer is repeated for each one by name.*

O God, according to the riches of your glory,
strengthen *(name)* in *his/her* inner being
with power through your Holy Spirit.
Grant that Christ may dwell in *his/her* heart
as *s/he* is being rooted and grounded in love.
Give *(name)* the grace to comprehend, with all your saints,
what is the breadth and length
and height and depth of the love of Christ,
and to know that love though it surpasses knowledge,
until *s/he* is filled with all the fullness of your Spirit.
  Amen.
—based on Ephesians 3:16–19

Dismissal
"Lead a life worthy of the calling to which you have been called,
with all humility and gentleness,
with patience, bearing with one another in love,
making every effort to maintain the unity of the Spirit in the bond of peace."
—Ephesians 4:1–2

Go in peace to be friends, friends in Christ and friends of Christ,
and to bear fruit that will last.

---

4. Adapted from the *Book of Common Worship*, 443.

Renewal of Baptism

For those Uniting with the Congregation

This liturgy is adapted from the 1993 Book of Common Worship of the Presbyterian Church (U.S.A.) (pp. 455–62 and 452). Congregations of other denominations will want to consult the appropriate liturgy from their own tradition, and/or from the congregation's customary practice.

The service takes place in Sunday worship, ordinarily following the reading and preaching of the Word and before the celebration of the Lord's Supper. Participants, including an elder representing the session, the new member, and his/her member companion, are invited to gather near the baptismal font, which shall be open and filled with water. If more than one new member is being received, the wording may be adjusted accordingly.

A previously baptized new member publicly professing faith for the first time may be received by adapting this liturgy or using another intended for such occasion. Those who have not been previously baptized are united with the congregation in a celebration of the sacrament of Baptism.

Presentation

> *An elder presents those whom the session has received by letter of transfer or by reaffirmation of faith.*

On behalf of the session,
I present *(name)*, who is received into the membership of this congregation by reaffirmation of his/her faith. Or, by transfer from _____ church.
His/her companion in prayer and conversation
over the past weeks has been *(name)*.

Renewal of Baptism

The minister addresses the new member:

(Name), you come to us as a member
of the one, holy, universal church
into which you were baptized
and by which you have been nurtured.
We rejoice in the gifts you bring to us.
We welcome you, not as a stranger in our midst
but as a *brother/sister* in Christ.

Hear what the Scriptures say:
"There is one body and one Spirit,
just as you were called to the one hope of your calling,
one Lord, one faith, one baptism,
one God . . . who is above all and through all and in all."

—*Ephesians 4:4–6*

Profession of Faith

*The minister addresses those assembled at the font
and the congregation.*

As you join with us in the worship and service of this congregation,
it is fitting that together we reaffirm
the covenant into which we were baptized,
claiming again the promises of God which are ours in baptism.
Therefore, I ask you:

Trusting in the gracious mercy of God,
do you turn from the ways of sin
and renounce evil and its power in the world?
> ***I do.***

Do you turn to Jesus Christ
and accept him as your Lord and Savior,
trusting in his grace and love?
> ***I do.***

APPENDIX

Will you be Christ's faithful disciple,
obeying his Word and showing his love?
   I will.* Or, *I will, with God's help.

Together with the whole church, let us confess our faith,
using the words of the Apostle's Creed *(the congregation standing)*:
   I believe in God, the Father Almighty, creator. . .

The minister continues, addressing the new member.

(Name), you have now publicly professed your faith.
Will you be a faithful member of this congregation?
Will you share in its worship and ministry
through your presence and your prayers,
your gifts, your study and your service,
and so fulfill your calling to be a disciple of Jesus Christ?
   I will.* Or, *I will, with God's help.

Prayers
Let us pray . . .

*The minister, or the member companion, offers one of
the following, or a similar prayer:*

(A)
Holy God, we praise you
for calling us to be a servant people.
and for gathering us into the body of Christ.
We thank you for choosing to add *(name)* to our number.
Together may we live in your Spirit,
and so love one another,
that we may have the mind of Jesus Christ our Lord,
to whom we give honor and glory forever.

*The following is especially appropriate for those who have not
participated in the life of the church for an extended period.*

(B)
Faithful God, you work in us and for us
even when we do not know it.
When our path has led us away from you,
you guide us back to yourself.
We thank you for calling your servant *(name)*
into the fellowship of your people.
Renew in *him/her* the covenant you made in *his/her* baptism.
Continue the good work you have begun in *him/her*.
Send *him/her* forth in the power of your Spirit,
to love and serve you with joy
and to strive for justice and peace in all the earth,
in the name of Jesus Christ our Lord.

Laying on of Hands

> *The minister, elder, and member companion may lay hands*
> *on the newcomer's head or shoulder during the prayer.*
> *If more than one new member is being received,*
> *the prayer is repeated for each one by name.*

O Lord, uphold *(name)* by your Holy Spirit.
Daily increase in *him/her* your gifts of grace:
the spirit of wisdom and understanding,
the spirit of counsel and might,
the spirit of knowledge and the fear of the Lord,
the spirit of joy in your presence,
both now and forever.
    Amen.

> *The minister concludes:*

Everliving God,
guard this your servant with your protecting hand,
and let your Holy Spirit be with *him/her* forever.

Lead *him/her* to know and obey your Word
that *s/he* may serve you in this life
and dwell with you forever in the life to come,
through Jesus Christ our Lord.
    Amen.

Welcome

The elder addresses the new member.

(Name), we welcome you to this congregation
and to its worship, discipleship and service.
Go in peace, to serve the Lord with us.

The minister, elder and member companion greet the new member.

The peace of Christ be with you.

Additional Conversation Guides

The pages that follow offer several conversation guides, using the Word–Share–Prayer format, on additional topics: Worship, Discipleship, Service, and Justice. These were developed for a congregation-wide faith-sharing event, and used along with several of the Word–Share–Prayer exercises from *Companions*. They might be used in other ways as well, but they are *not* intended to be substituted for, or added to, any of the eight *Companions* conversations in the church's ministry with newcomers.

Worship

WORD: Read Isaiah 6:1–8

> In the year that King Uzziah died, I saw the Lord sitting on a throne high and lofty; and the hem of his robe filled the temple. Seraphs were in attendance above him; each had six wings: with two they covered their faces, and with two they covered their feet, and with two they flew. And one called to another and said: "Holy, holy, holy is the Lord of hosts; the whole earth is full of his glory." The pivots on the thresholds shook at the voices of those who called, and the house filled with smoke. And I said, "Woe is me! I am lost, for I am a man of unclean lips, and I live among a people of unclean lips; yet my eyes have seen the King, the Lord of hosts!" Then one of the seraphs flew to me, holding a live coal that had been taken from the altar with a pair of tongs. The seraph touched my mouth with it and said, "Now that this has touched your lips, your guilt has departed and your sin is blotted out." Then I heard the voice of the Lord saying, "Whom shall I send, and who will go for us?" And I said, "Here am I; send me!" (NRSV)

SHARE

In Isaiah's experience, there is awe for the sheer majesty and mystery of God. Where do you experience *awe* in the worship of the church? In other places?

What other elements of our worship do you identify in Isaiah's experience?

Look at a Sunday morning bulletin and talk about the parts of worship that touch you, draw you close to God, confuse you, frustrate you, engage you, bore you, challenge you, inspire you, etc.

Our worship follows an ancient pattern where the two main acts of hearing the Word and giving thanks around the Table are bracketed by a gathering in and a sending out. What does this pattern mean to you? Does it help you in your living to listen more? be more grateful? something else?

We have ministers to preach and celebrate sacraments, but worship (liturgy) is literally "the work of the people." What ways of participating in the church's worship mean the most to you? Why?

PRAYER

Share any needs or joys for prayer.
Pray for each other, especially around the things you have shared today.
You may want to end with this song of praise from Psalm 100:

> *Be joyful in the Lord, all you lands; serve the Lord with gladness and come before God's presence with a song. Know this: The Lord alone is God; we belong to the Lord who made us, we are God's people and the sheep of God's pasture. Enter God's gates with thanksgiving; go into the holy courts with praise; give thanks and call upon the name of the Lord. For good is the Lord, whose mercy is everlasting; and whose faithfulness endures from age to age.*

Discipleship

WORD: Read Mark 1:14-20

> Now after John was arrested, Jesus came to Galilee, proclaiming the good news of God and saying, "The time is fulfilled, and the kingdom of God has come near; repent, and believe in the good news." As Jesus passed along the Sea of Galilee, he saw Simon and his brother Andrew casting a net into the sea—for they were fishermen. And Jesus said to them, "Follow me, and I will make you fish for people." And immediately they left their nets and followed him. As he went a little farther, he saw James son of Zebedee and his brother John, who were in their boat mending the nets. Immediately he called them; and they left their father Zebedee in the boat with the hired men, and followed him. (NRSV)

SHARE

This is the classic pattern of disciples being drawn to a rabbi's message and signing on to learn from his teaching and follow his way of life. What teachings of Jesus have convinced you, that *you* want to be *his* disciple?

How do you keep learning in your faith? Is that something you pursue alone? Or with others? At our church? Or in other learning settings? In a disciplined way? Or more occasionally?

Describe a discipleship/learning experience that really excited you and helped you grow as a Christian. What made that experience so powerful for you?

Being a disciple in Jesus' day was more like being an apprentice than a student. What might you do differently, if you thought of yourself as an apprentice learning from Jesus a new way of life?

Jesus connected *being* a disciple with *making* disciples. Why might that connection be important? How do the two go together for you?

PRAYER

Share any special needs and pray for each other.
You may want to conclude with this prayer based on Ephesians 3:16-19:

> *O God, according to the riches of your glory, strengthen _____ and me in our inner being with power through your Holy Spirit. Grant that Christ may dwell in our hearts as we are being rooted and grounded in love. Give us the grace to comprehend, with all your saints, what is the breadth and length and height and depth of the love of Christ, and to know that love, though it surpasses knowledge, until we are filled with all the fullness of your Spirit. Amen.*

Service

WORD: Read Matthew 25:32–40

> "All the nations will be gathered before the Son of Man, and he will separate the people one from another as a shepherd separates the sheep from the goats. He will put the sheep on his right and the goats on his left. Then the King will say to those on his right, 'Come, you who are blessed by my Father: take your inheritance, the kingdom prepared for you since the creation of the world. For I was hungry and you gave me something to eat. I was thirsty and you gave me something to drink. I was a stranger and you invited me in. I needed clothes and you clothed me, I was sick and you looked after me, I was in prison and you came to visit me.' Then the righteous will answer him, 'Lord, when did we see you hungry and feed you, or thirsty and give you something to drink? When did we see you a stranger and invite you in, or needing clothes and clothe you? When did we see you sick or in prison and go to visit you?' The King will reply, 'Truly I tell you, whatever you did for one of the least of these brothers and sisters of mine, you did for me.'" (TNIV)

SHARE

There are all kinds of places God calls us to serve. Where are you involved with serving others? The hungry? The sick? Strangers? Clothing? Housing? Refugees? Prisons? Education? The arts? The earth?

Is there anyplace where you are engaged in service that you makes you feel like you are serving Jesus himself? Where?

Is your service to others an expression of your faith in Christ? In what ways?

Have you ever been involved in a form of service that you know you don't want to do again? What did you learn from that experience about yourself? about God?

Has the way you serve others changed or evolved over time? What kind of service did you used to do, that you no longer do now? Is there a way of serving you've never tried but want to?

Acts of service help others, but they also change the server. What gifts or insights has serving given you? Why do you think Jesus was so insistent on his followers being servants of others?

PRAYER

See if your companion has particular needs for prayer today.
Pray for each other, especially around the things you have shared today.
You may want to conclude with the Lord's Prayer together.

Justice

WORD: Read Amos 5:21–24

> I hate, I despise your festivals, and I take no delight in your solemn assemblies. Even though you offer me your burnt offerings and grain offerings, I will not accept them; and the offerings of well-being of your fatted animals I will not look upon. Take away from me the noise of your songs; I will not listen to the melody of your harps. But let justice roll down like waters, and righteousness like an ever-flowing stream. (NRSV)

SHARE

Do Christians today, like the ancient Israelites, sometimes overlook justice in order to focus on more "spiritual" matters? Where do you see that happening—in the church? in yourself?

Can worship deepen our desire to live and work for justice in the world? Where have you experienced that?

Can you identify with the prophet's hope for "justice rolling down like waters"? What injustice in the world do you most long to see set right?

In what ways do you work for justice, now or in the past? Have some of those efforts been rewarding? Frustrating? What keeps you going? Has the church been a source of support?

Many Christians believe that politics have no place in the church. What do you think Amos would say about that? Or Jesus? How do *you* draw the lines between your politics and your faith? Where do those lines cross?

Alongside witness, worship, and spiritual nurture, the church is committed to what earlier generations called "the promotion of social righteousness." What does that mean to you?

PRAYER

Share any special needs.
Pray for each other, and for the world.
You may want to conclude with this prayer of St. Francis of Assisi:

> *Lord, make me an instrument of your peace.*
> *Where there is hatred, let me sow love; where there is injury, pardon;*
> *where there is doubt, faith; where there is despair, hope;*
> *where there is darkness, light; and where there is sadness, joy. Amen.*

Bibliography

Buechner, Frederick. *Wishful Thinking: A Theological ABC*. New York: Harper & Row, 1973.

Hainer, Frank T. "The One Story of the Bible." In *New Ventures in Bible Study*, 65–85. Crawfordsville, IN: Geneva, 1980.

Johnson, Ben Campbell. *Speaking of God: Evangelism as Initial Spiritual Guidance*. Louisville: Westminster/John Knox, 1991.

Ott, E. Stanley. *Transform Your Church with Ministry Teams*. Grand Rapids: Eerdmans, 2004. See pages 100–103 and 176–82.

Peterson, Eugene H. "Lectio Divina." In *Eat This Book: A Conversation in the Art of Spiritual Reading*, 79–118. Grand Rapids: Eerdmans, 2006.

Presbyterian Church (U.S.A.). *Book of Common Worship*. Louisville: Westminster/John Knox, 1993.

Roush, Bart. "Incorporating Adults towards a Missional Imagination: A Study of Four Congregations." DMin diss., Luther Seminary, St. Paul, 2012.

Thompson, Marjorie J. "Chewing the Bread of the Word: the Nature and Practice of Spiritual Reading." In *SoulFeast: An Invitation to the Christian Spiritual Life*, 17–30. Louisville: Westminster/John Knox, 1995.

Wheatley, Margaret J. *Turning to One Another: Simple Conversations to Restore Hope to the Future*. San Francisco: Berrett-Koehler, 2002.

Made in the USA
Middletown, DE
13 September 2018